Generative Adversarial Networks with Industrial Use Cases

*Learning How to Build GAN
Applications for Retail, Healthcare,
Telecom, Media, Education, and HRTech*

by

Navin K. Manaswi

FIRST EDITION 2020

Copyright © BPB Publications, India

ISBN: 978-93-89423-853

Distributors:

BPB PUBLICATIONS
20, Ansari Road, Darya Ganj
New Delhi-110002
Ph: 23254990/23254991

DECCAN AGENCIES
4-3-329, Bank Street,
Hyderabad-500195
Ph: 24756967/24756400

MICRO MEDIA
Shop No. 5, Mahendra Chambers,
150 DN Rd. Next to Capital Cinema,
V.T. (C.S.T.) Station, MUMBAI-400 001
Ph: 22078296/22078297

BPB BOOK CENTRE
376 Old Lajpat Rai Market,
Delhi-110006
Ph: 23861747

Published by Manish Jain for BPB Publications, 20 Ansari Road, Darya Ganj, New Delhi-110002 and Printed at Repro India Ltd, Mumbai

Dedicated to

The family that offers immense love to energize me

About the Author

Navin K Manaswi has been developing AI solutions/products for HRTech, Retail, ITSM, Healthcare, Telecom, Insurance, Digital Marketing, and Supply Chain while working for Consulting companies in Malaysia, Singapore, and Dubai. He is a serial entrepreneur in Artificial Intelligence and Augmented Reality Space. He has been building solutions for video intelligence, document intelligence, and human-like chatbots. He is a Guest Faculty at IIT Kharagpur for AI Course and an author of the famous book on deep learning. He is officially a Google Developer Expert in machine learning. He has been organizing and mentoring AI hackathons and boot camps at Google events and college events. His startup WoWExp has been building awesome products in AI and AR space.

Acknowledgement

I want to thank the great support which I have got from my family and friends. I thank my mother, father, brother (Satish) and sister (Divya) for their morale-boosting. I thank my spouse (Anita) and kid (Pramsu) for tolerating me while I was spending a huge amount of time writing and editing the book.

I would like to thank my WoW Exp team for their support. Special thanks to Trilok and Chirag.

Finally, I would like to thank Anugraha and Sourabh at BPB Publications for giving me this opportunity to write my book for them.

Preface

Having worked in Industry for many years, I realized the importance of fast learning. Artificial Intelligence is one of the most prominent skills-in-demand in almost all industries. For the last 5 years, millions of students and professionals have made an entry into the Artificial Intelligence space. We can confidently say that millions of people want to upgrade their skills in deep learning, especially advanced deep learning. If you are one of them, this book is meant for you. This book would also help all students, professors, researchers, and technical professionals who work to develop advanced deep learning codes, specially GAN codes across verticals. Industry professionals from healthcare backgrounds would find many use cases and codes, approaches, and details of related GAN applications. Even people with Retail experience would find codes, applications, and details of related GAN applications. EduTech Professionals learn to develop codes and applications. This book would also help people from HRTech, Telecom, and Media & Entertainment fields.

First chapter focuses on explaining the overall deep learning landscape and GAN's relevance in the world of deep learning. It also explains deep learning in simple words using a visual description. It demonstrates how to build the codes for basic GAN applications.

Second chapter discusses GAN applications across industries. It explains relevant GAN papers for Retail, Telecom, Media & Entertainment, HRTech, Autonomous vehicles.

Third chapter goes into details of mathematics of GAN. It explains the basic mathematical units of GAN and illustrates and explains KL divergence and JS divergence, the very foundation of GAN. It also explains Nash equilibrium, Mode collapse, and other nitty-gritty of GAN.

Fourth and last chapter explains important kinds of GAN, such as conditional GAN, DCGAN, pix2pix GAN, Style GAN, and cycle GAN.

I personally believe that this book will serve the purpose of AI researchers and professionals across the globe and across industries. I wish you the best in your learning endeavors

Errata

We take immense pride in our work at BPB Publications and follow best practices to ensure the accuracy of our content to provide with an indulging reading experience to our subscribers. Our readers are our mirrors, and we use their inputs to reflect and improve upon human errors if any, occurred during the publishing processes involved. To let us maintain the quality and help us reach out to any readers who might be having difficulties due to any unforeseen errors, please write to us at :

errata@bpbonline.com

Your support, suggestions and feedbacks are highly appreciated by the BPB Publications' Family.

Table of Contents

Chapter 1
Basics of Generative Adversarial Networks (GAN)

Introduction

Deep learning has been the greatest idea of **Artificial Intelligence (AI)**. It not only solves very complex problems, but also automates many mundane tasks of the industries. Autonomous vehicles, medical imaging and e-commerce have been obsessed with deep learning for all good reasons. To make the deep learning applications comprehensible, we have listed down types of deep learning tasks. **Generative Adversarial Networks (GANs)** are one of the hottest topics in deep learning. They can generate an infinite number of similar images samples based on a given dataset. The underlying idea behind GAN is that it contains two neural networks that compete against each other in a zero-sum game framework, that is a generator and a discriminator.

Structure

- Layman's perspective and its architecture
- How to build the code for GAN from scratch

Objectives

Illustration of GAN and teaching how to write code for GAN.

Deep learning applications at a glance

Deep learning has been used for every kind of AI applications. We need to understand the kinds of deep learning applications and deep learning frameworks before jumping on GAN.

Types of deep learning applications

Image classification

Image classification is a supervised learning problem, this means that the set of target classes (objects to identify in images) and the set of training classes are labelled, and the model is trained using the training set to recognize the objects of the test set. Early computer vision models relied on raw pixel data as the input to the model. Raw pixel data alone doesn't provide a sufficiently stable representation to encompass the myriad variations of an object as captured in an image. The position of the object, background behind the object, ambient lighting, camera angle, and camera focus all can produce a fluctuation in raw pixel data; these differences are significant enough that they cannot be corrected by taking weighted averages of pixel RGB values. The bottleneck of this approach results in a heavy load on feature engineering.

Improvement in image classification came with the discovery of **Convolutional Neural Network (CNN),** which could be used to extract higher-level representations of image content. CNN is a class of deep learning neural networks. They are specifically designed to analyze visual imagery and are frequently working behind the scenes in image classification. They can be found at the core of everything from Facebook's photo tagging to self-driving cars.

In CNN instead of feeding the entire image as an array of numbers, the image is broken up into a number of tiles, the machine then tries to predict what each tile is. Finally, the computer tries to predict what's in the picture based on the prediction of all the tiles. This allows the computer to parallelize the operations and detect the object regardless of where it is located in the image. A CNN has an input layer, an output layer and hidden layers which usually consists of:

- **Convolutional layers:** It appliesa convolution operation to the input. This passes the information on to the next layer.

- **ReLU layers:** This is an activation layer, which introduces non-linearity in the features.

- **Pooling layers:** It combines the outputs of clusters of neurons into a single neuron in the next layer.

- **A fully connected layer:** It connects every neuron in one layer to every neuron in the next layer.

CNN works by extracting features from images. This eliminates the need for manual feature extraction. The features are not trained! They're learned while the network trains on a set of images. This makes deep learning models extremely accurate for computer vision tasks. CNNs learn feature detection through tens or hundreds of hidden layers. Each layer increases the complexity of the learned features.

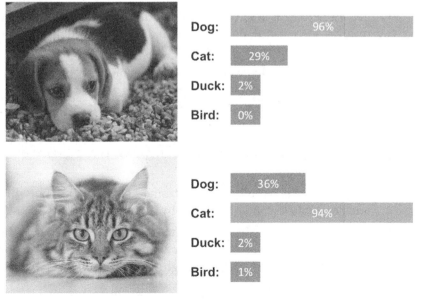

Figure 1.1

Semantic segmentation

Segmentation is essential for image analysis tasks. Semantic segmentation describes the process of associating each pixel of an image with a class label. It is one of the high-level tasks that paves the way towards complete scene understanding.

Applications for semantic segmentation include:

- Autonomous driving
- Virtual reality
- Industrial inspection
- Classification of terrain visible in satellite imagery
- Medical imaging analysis

With the popularity of deep learning in recent years, many semantic segmentation problems are being tackled using deep architectures, most often CNNs, which exceeded other approaches by a large margin in terms of accuracy and efficiency.

Semantic segmentation is a natural step in the progression from coarse to fine inference at pixel level:

- The origin could be located at classification, which consists of making a prediction for a whole input.
- The next step is **localization/detection**, which provides not only the classes but also additional information regarding the spatial location of those classes.
- Finally, semantic segmentation achieves fine-grained inference by making dense predictions inferring labels for every pixel so that each pixel is labelled with the class of its enclosing object ore region.

The architecture of semantic segmentation model is comprised of an encoder and a decoder:

- The encoder is usually is a pre-trained classification network such as VGG/ResNet followed by a decoder network.
- The task of the decoder is to semantically project the discriminative features (lower resolution) learnt by the encoder onto the pixel space (higher resolution) to get a dense classification.

- Simply stretching the pixels in an image based on the output dimension may result in an inappropriate image, there are some techniques which are used to enlarge the image. Let's see how it might look if we want to create a 4*4 image by using 2*2 input.

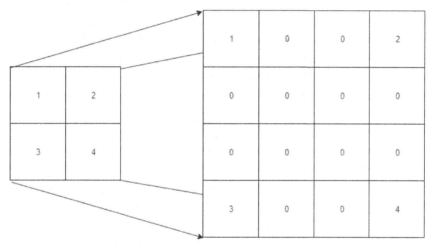

Figure 1.2

Resizing the image to its original pixel is also called **upsampling,** there are various techniques to the upsampling show below, nearest neighbours: rather than performing complex mathematical operation this method takes the pixel value from the nearest pixel and resize the image.

- **Bilinear interpolation:** In this approach, we calculate the weighted distance between each nearest pixel using linear interpolation and calculate the new pixel.

- **Bicubic interpolation:** We chooses the nearest pixel in this approach as well, but instead of linear interpolation to calculate the new pixel value like above here we have to choose 3rd order polynomial interpolation, this takes somewhat more time than the other two methods but gives better and smoother results.

Semantic segmentation requires discrimination at pixel and projects those discriminative features learnt at different stages of the encoder onto the pixel space.

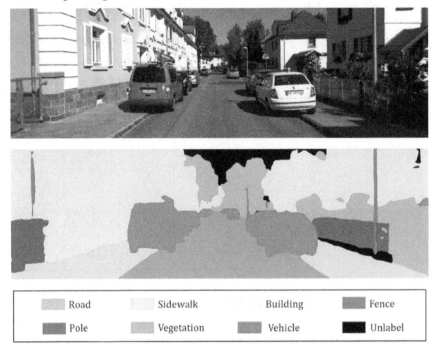

Figure 1.3

Semantic search

Semantic search is when a whole lot of resources are used in order to perform a search, rather than just keywords.

Semantic search describes a search engine's attempt to generate the most accurate results possible by understanding:

- Searcher intent
- Query context
- The relationships between words

In layman's terms, semantic search seeks to understand natural language the way a human would. We can search content for its meaning in addition to keywords, and maximize the chances the user will find the information they are looking for.

The purpose of semantic search is to go beyond the static dictionary meaning of a word or phrase to understand the intent of a searcher's query within a specific context. By learning from past results and creating links between entities, a search engine might then be able to deduce the answer to a searcher's query, rather than provide ten blue links that may or may not provide the correct answer.

For identifying best results, web search relies on characteristics of web pages (features) such as the number of keyword matches between the query and the web page's title, URL, body text and so on. defined by engineers (just an example). During run time, these features are fed into classical machine learning models like gradient boosted trees to rank web pages. Each query-web page pair becomes the fundamental unit of ranking

Deep learning improves this process by allowing us to automatically generate additional features that more comprehensively capture the intent of the query and the characteristics of a webpage.

Specifically, unlike human-defined and term-based matching features, these new features learned by deep learning models can better capture the meaning of phrases missed by traditional keyword matching. This improved understanding of natural language (that is, semantic understanding) is inferred from end-user clicks on webpages for a search query. The deep learning features represent each text-based query and webpage as a string of numbers known as the query vector and document vector, respectively.

These query and web page vectors are fed into a deep model known as the **convolutional neural network (CNN)**. This model improves semantic understanding and generalization between query and webpages and calculates the output score for ranking. It is achieved by measuring the similarity between a query and a webpage's title, URL and so on, using a distance metric, for example, cosine similarity.

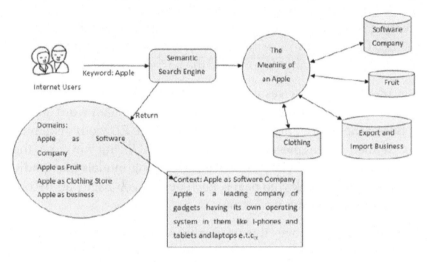

Figure 1.4

Text classification

Text classification describes a general class of problems such as predicting the sentiment of tweets and movie reviews, as well as classifying email as spam or not. It is a part of **natural language processing (NLP)** and **supervised machine learning (ML),** it's an example of supervised machine learning task since a labelled dataset containing text documents, and their labels areused for training a classifier. The goal of text classification is to automatically classify the text documents into one or more predefined categories. Deep learning methods are proving very good at text classification, achieving state-of-the-art results on a suite of standard academic benchmark problems.

The deep neural network model for text classification involves the use of a word embedding for representing words and a CNN for learning how to discriminate documents on classification problems. CNN is a class of deep, feed-forward artificial neural networks (where connections between nodes do not form a cycle) and uses a variation of multilayer perceptrons designed to require minimal preprocessing. These are inspired by animal visual cortex.

CNNs are generally used in computer vision;however, they've recently been applied to various NLP tasks, and the results were promising.

The architecture of the text classification model has three major parts:

- **Word embedding:** A distributed representation of words where different words that have a similar meaning (based on their usage) also have a similar representation.

- **Convolutional model:** A feature extraction model that learns to extract salient features from documents represented using a word embedding.

- **Fully connected model:** The interpretation of extracted features in terms of a predictive output.

There are other deep learning models also which are used for text classification such as a **recurrent neural network (RNN), hierarchical attention network (HAN),** and so on but CNN outperforms all the other models.

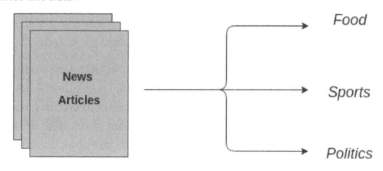

Figure 1.5

/// This above figure shows an example where using RNN the News Articles can be classified to different classes.

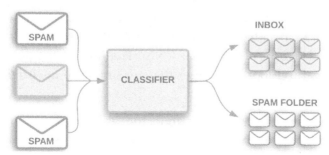

Figure 1.6

Generating images

GANs are one of the hottest topics in deep learning. They can generate an infinite number of similarimage samples based on a given dataset. The underlying idea behind GAN is that it contains two neural networks that compete against each other in a zero-sum game framework, that is, generator and a discriminator.

Generator

The generator takes random noise as an input and generates samples as an output. Its goal is to generate such samples that will fool the discriminator to think that it sees real images while actually seeing fakes. We can think of the generator as a counterfeit.

Discriminator

Discriminator takes both real images from the input dataset and fake images from the generator and outputs a verdict whether a given image is legit or not. We can think of the discriminator as a policeman trying to catch the bad guys while letting the good guys free.

The discriminator has the task of determining whether a given image looks natural (that is, is an image from the dataset) or looks like it has been artificially created. The task of the generator is to create natural-looking images that are similar to the original data distribution, images that look natural enough to fool the discriminator network. Firstly a random noise is given to the generator;using this it creates the fake images and then these fake images are along with original images sent to the discriminator.

The discriminative model has the task of determining whether a given image looks natural (an image from the dataset) or looks like it has been artificially created. This is basically a binary classifier that will take the form of a normal CNN. The task of the generator is to create natural-looking images that are similar to the original data distribution.

The generator is trying to fool the discriminator while the discriminator is trying not to get fooled by the generator. As the models train through alternating optimization, both methods are improved until a point where the fake images are indistinguishable from the dataset images.

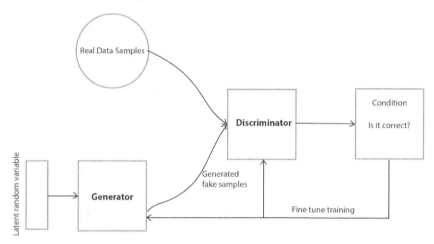

Figure 1.7

Figure 1.8

Object detection

An image classification problem is predicting the label of an image among the predefined labels. It assumes that there is a single object of interest in the image, and it covers a significant portion of the image. Detection is about not only finding the class of object but also localizing the extent of an object in the image.

This object detection is the procedure of determining the instance of the class to which the object belongs and estimating the location of the object by outputting the bounding box around the object. Detecting a single instance of a class from an image is called as **single class object detection**, whereas detecting the classes of all objects present in the image is known as multi-class object detection. Different challenges, such as partial/full occlusion, varying illumination conditions, poses, scale, and so on. are needed to be handled while performing object detection.

There are many approaches toobject detection:

- Naïve way (divide and conquer)
- Increase the number of divisions
- Performing structured divisions
- Using deep learning for feature selection and to build an end-to-end approach

Of all the preceding methods, deep learning is the most efficient way. Object detection is modelled as a classification problem where we take windows of fixed sizes from input image at all the possible locations to feed these patches to an image classifier. Each window is fed to the classifier which predicts the class of the object in the window (or background if none is present). Hence, we know both the class and location of the objects in the image.

Figure 1.9

Figure 1.10

Multi-variate time series prediction

Real-world time series forecasting is challenging for a whole host of reasons not limited to problem features such as having multiple input variables, the requirement to predict multiple time steps, and the need to perform the same type of prediction for multiple physical sites.

There are two types of time series prediction:

- **Univariate time series prediction:** A univariate time series prediction problem will have only two variables. One is date-time, and the other is the field on which prediction is to be done.

- **Multivariate time series prediction:** A multivariate time series prediction problem will have more than two variables.

One is date-time, one is the field on which prediction is to be done, and other fields depicts the scenarios which will affect the prediction. It typically involves the prediction of single or multiple values from multi-variate input that are typically interconnected through some event.

Multivariate time series data are ubiquitous in many practical applications ranging from health care, geoscience, astronomy, to biology and others. They often inevitably carry missing observations due to various reasons, such as medical events, saving costs, anomalies, inconvenience, and so on. It has been noted that these missing values are usually **Informative Missingness;** that is, the missing values and patterns provide rich information about target labels in supervised learning tasks.

There are many approaches to deal with the missing values in time series, a simple solution is to omit the missing data and to perform the analysis only on the observed data, but it does not provide good performance when the missing rate is high and inadequate samples are kept. Another solution is to fill in the missing values with substituted values, which is known as **data imputation**. However, these methods do not capture variable correlations and may not capture complex pattern to perform imputation. Recently, RNN, such as **long short-term memory (LSTM)** and **gated recurrent unit (GRU),** have shown to achieve the state-of-the-art results in many applications with time series prediction. RNNs enjoy several nice properties such as strong prediction performance as well as the ability to capture long-term temporal dependencies and variable-length observations.

LSTM, which are one of the RNN, has the capability of handling huge data. The deep learning models also have the support of learning in batches, saving, and reusing them with the new data to continue the training process.

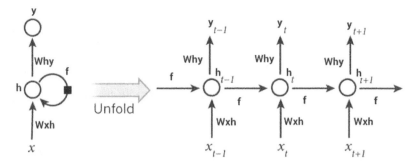

Figure 1.11

Information extraction from the scan

The extraction of relevant information from unstructured documents can be used in many different applications. **Named entity recognition (NER)** is a specific task of information extraction. It aims at the identification of named entities such as persons, locations, organizations, dates,and so on in the text. The automatic labelling of a NER system can be used by publishers, libraries, or other content providers to tag documents and potentially improve search results. Other obvious applications are recommendation systems and customer support.

A potential solution to this generalization problem is the use of statistical models based on **machine learning (ML).** One of the most successful ML methods before the resurrection of neural networks were models based on **conditional random fields (CRF).** The performance of these models heavily depended on hand-crafted features which require a lot of domain-specific knowledge and often a deep understanding of linguistics.

In recent years the development in this area has been dominated by **deep learning (DL)** methods. DL models are usually trained end-to-end, that is, extensive manual feature engineering is not required any more. The lower layers of the deep neural network learn the optimal feature representation by itself, while the higher layers act as the final classifier. The challenge nowadays is merely the choice or the construction of the right network architecture, the definition of an appropriate cost function and the gathering of a lot of data.

RNN has been the preferred choice of DL architectures for the NER task amongst researchers and practitioners. In particular, RNNs based on LSTM cells or GRU cells. Recently, also models based on one-dimensional CNN, the so-called **Temporal CNN (TCN)** are reported to give competitive results. Currently, the most successful architectures often consist of a multi-layer RNN or TCN with a CRF as the final layer.

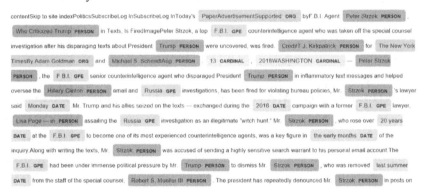

Figure 1.12

Different deep learning frameworks

1. **Sci-kit learn:** Sklearn is one of the widely used frameworks, and it is very popular for classic machine learning techniques for supervised and unsupervised learning. It is widely known for its simplicity which lets users get the desired output in just a few lines of code. You can use many ML models such as Random Forest, SVM and many more by following pretty intuitive steps. It doesn't support Neural Networks and GPU.

2. **Caffee:** Caffee was probably the first deep learning library started in 2013, but it was not flexible. In Caffee you have to define full forward-backwards update for each node, you also have to write different lines of code for CPU and GPU, you also have to define the model in a plain text editor! It was very popular when it was released, but since then, many things in the deep learning community improved.

3. **Keras:** Keras is one of the most widely used high level deep learning frameworks to start with, it is also so much simpler to use, and it supports GPU as well, it sits on top of other libraries such as TensorFlow, it uses an object-oriented design, so everything inside of it is considered an object.

4. **Theano:** Theano was an open-source project developed by LISA group from Montreal, it has got so much attention and was good at implementing deep learning models, it also generates a computational graph and perform automatic differentiation, it uses to outperform TensorFlow on a single GPU. Code to implement Theano is not cleaner as compared to TensorFlow.

5. **Pytorch:** Pytorch is also the popular deep learning framework, it also runs on Python, it provides tensor computations, its Autograd function builds computation graphs from tensors and automatically computes gradients. We can also change the computational graphs in runtime!

Introduction to GAN

Figure 1.13

Welcome !!! It is always a great idea to get a story from a picture. Here is a story where a forger is quite smart. He sells the fake milk and milk shop-owner can tell that it is fake. The forger is smart as he starts learning from feedback given by shop-owner. Every next time, he produces a bit less fake milk and learns from feedback. Eventually, the forger would be able to oversmart the shop owner. The forger, finally, generates the milk as close as real milk.

Congratulations!!! You have understood GAN. Here the forger is the generator, and the shop-owner is the discriminator. GAN consists of two deep learning models, one generator model and one discriminator model. In short, we can summarize GAN as follows

1. Generator(forger) generates / creates / manufactures milk and
2. Discriminator(milk shop-owner / expert person who knows real milk and fake milk)
3. In the first go, generator (forger) generates milk and discriminator (milk shop-owner) can tell that this is fake. Learning from feedback / loss function, the forger (generator) improves next time, again discriminator tells that this is fake, but this fake would be less fake than the first one. In this way, feedback helps the forger improve the milk quality until the time discriminator says that the milk is real.

   a. Let us come to the formal look

GAN architecture and explanation

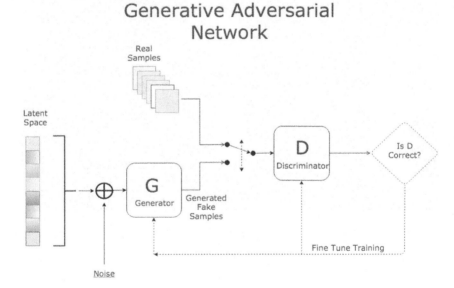

Generative Adversarial Network

Figure 1.14

GANs or **Generative Adversarial Networks** is a framework for estimating generative models. Two models are trained simultaneously by an adversarial process: a generator, which is responsible for generating data , and a discriminator, which is responsible for estimating the probability that an image was drawn from the training data (the image is real), or was produced by the generator (the image is fake). During training, the generator becomes progressively better at generating images, until the discriminator is no longer able to distinguish real images from fake.

GAN is inspired by the zero-sum non-cooperative game. It means that if one wins, the other loses. A zero-sum game is also known as **minimax**. Player A wants to maximize its actions, but player B want to minimize them. In-game theory, the GAN model converges when the discriminator (player A) and the generator (player B) reach Nash equilibrium. This is the optimal point for the minimax equation.

Training GAN is equivalent to minimizing JS divergence (or KL divergence) between probability distribution q (estimated distribution, from a generator) and probability distribution p (the real-life distribution). In layman's words, JS divergence (or KL divergence) represents the distance between two probability distribution functions.

Getting started with GAN

Let us try to do a task on GAN.

Task

Here we are trying to generate new (look-like) celebrity faces using GANs given that we have many known celebrity faces.

Dataset

The CelebA dataset is the public dataset of collection of over 200,000 celebrity faces.

You can google CelebA dataset that is a **Large-scale CelebFaces Attributes** (CelebA) Dataset

CelebA is a large-scale face attributes dataset with more than 2,00,000 celebrity images, each with 40 attribute annotations. The images in this dataset cover large pose variations and background clutter.

Data extraction

You can either upload the zip file (of CelebA dataset) on colab and unzip it there and else you can use helper function for data extraction.

```
------------------------------------------
import helper
helper.download_extract('celeba', '/content')
------------------------------------------
```

Preprocessing the images

We need to make sure all our input images are of the same size. We can simply resize the training data images to 28x28 image.

```
------------------------------------------------
width = 28
height = 28
image = image.resize([width, height])
------------------------------------------------
```

Architecture of generator

#Part 1

The generator architecture has the first dense layer and fully connected layer after that.

```
-----------------------------------------------------------
#creating a deep learning model architecture (Sequential
model)
# creating a dense layer having 7*7*512 nodes
    # batch normalization for normalization
# Passing through activation function named Leaky ReLu,
finer version of ReLu
def make_generator_model():

    model = tf.keras.Sequential()
model.add(tf.keras.layers.Dense(7*7*256, use_bias=False,
input_shape=(100,)))
model.add(tf.keras.layers.BatchNormalization())
model.add(tf.keras.layers.LeakyReLU())

model.add(tf.keras.layers.Reshape((7, 7, 256)))
```

```
assert model.output_shape == (None, 7, 7, 256)
# Note: None is the batch size
```

Part 2

The network architecture for the generator consists of Conv2DTranspose (upsampling) layers. We increase the width and height and reduce the depth as we move through the layers in the network. We use LeakyReLU activation for each layer except for the last one where we use a tanh activation.

```
model.add(tf.keras.layers.Conv2DTranspose(128, (3, 3),
strides=(1, 1), padding='same', use_bias=False))
    assert model.output_shape == (None, 7, 7, 128)
model.add(tf.keras.layers.BatchNormalization())
model.add(tf.keras.layers.LeakyReLU())

model.add(tf.keras.layers.Conv2DTranspose(64, (3, 3),
strides=(2, 2), padding='same', use_bias=False))
    assert model.output_shape == (None, 14, 14, 64)
model.add(tf.keras.layers.BatchNormalization())
model.add(tf.keras.layers.LeakyReLU())

model.add(tf.keras.layers.Conv2DTranspose(32, (3, 3),
strides=(2, 2), padding='same', use_bias=False))
    assert model.output_shape == (None, 28, 28, 32)
model.add(tf.keras.layers.BatchNormalization())
model.add(tf.keras.layers.LeakyReLU())
    print(model.summary)

model.add(tf.keras.layers.Conv2D(1, (3, 3), strides=(1,
1), padding='same', use_bias=False, activation='tanh'))
    print(model.summary)
    assert model.output_shape == (None, 28, 28, 1)

    return mode
```

Architecture of discriminator

The discriminator is responsible for distinguishing fake images from real images. It's similar to a regular CNN-based image classifier.

A discriminator is also the four-layer CNN with BatchNormalization and LeakyReLUlayer (except in input layer). The discriminator receives the output image (which is of size 28*28*3) and performs convolutions on it. At last,discriminator shows the output probabilities for showing whether the image is real or fake.

```python
def make_discriminator_model():
    model = tf.keras.Sequential()
model.add(tf.keras.layers.Conv2D(16, (3, 3), strides=(2, 2), padding='same', input_shape=[28, 28, 1]))

model.add(tf.keras.layers.LeakyReLU())

model.add(tf.keras.layers.Dropout(0.3))

model.add(tf.keras.layers.Conv2D(32, (3, 3), strides=(2, 2), padding='same'))

model.add(tf.keras.layers.LeakyReLU())

model.add(tf.keras.layers.Dropout(0.3))

model.add(tf.keras.layers.Conv2D(64, (3, 3), strides=(2, 2), padding='same'))

model.add(tf.keras.layers.LeakyReLU())

model.add(tf.keras.layers.Dropout(0.3))

model.add(tf.keras.layers.Conv2D(128, (3, 3), strides=(2, 2), padding='same'))

model.add(tf.keras.layers.LeakyReLU())

model.add(tf.keras.layers.Dropout(0.3))

model.add(tf.keras.layers.Flatten())

model.add(tf.keras.layers.Dense(1))

    return model


# Use the (as yet untrained) discriminator to classify the
generated images as real or fake. The model will be trained
to output positive values for real images and negative
values for fake images.
```

```
discriminator = make_discriminator_model()
decision = discriminator(generated_image)
```

Noise

The noise parameter is taken as input by the generator for generating the fake images. We can take a vector of random numbers to be our noise or z vector.

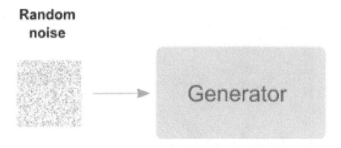

Figure 1.15

```
------------------
generator = make_generator_model()
noise = tf.random.normal([1, 100])
generated_image = generator(noise, training=False)
----------------------
```

It is then fed into a generator network for producing fake/noisy images.

Meanwhile, the generated image that is the fake image is given as an input to the discriminator model.

```
-----------------------------------------
discriminator = make_discriminator_model()
decision = discriminator(generated_image)
```

Loss

$$\min_{G} \max_{D} V(D, G) = \mathbb{E}_{x \sim p_{\text{data}}(x)}[\log D(x)] + \mathbb{E}_{z \sim p_z(z)}[\log(1 - D(G(z)))].$$

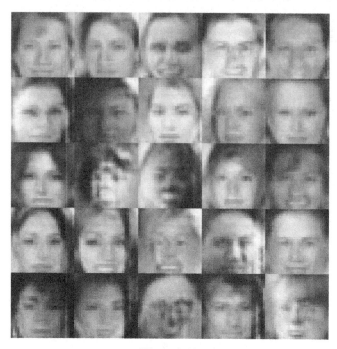

Figure 1.16

This is the original equation from the first-ever GAN paper published by *Ian Goodfellow*.

This equation shows the loss on which GANs work. It simply states that we need to minimize generator loss and maximize discriminator loss.

Vanishing gradient and mode collapse are two major issues of GAN. Vanishing gradient means the gradient is almost zero, so there is no major update in the weight of the neural networks while tuning. Mode collapse means that GAN keeps creating the same type of mode/image(same face, same flower,and so on).

How does it work?

So basically GAN consists of two losses one is generator loss; another is discriminator loss.What happens inside is that the generator tries to fool the discriminator by generating fake images. On the other hand, discriminator tries to compare the fake image passed on by generator with the real image data set. Generator here tries to manipulate then noise image in such a way that discriminator identify it as a real image while on the other side discriminator only agrees with an image whose feature vector is very much similar to the feature vector of the images in the data set.

- **Losses**

  We are strictly taking a loss to be of type `BinaryCrossentropy` because there are only 2 possibilities for an image that is,real or fake.

  ```
  cross_entropy = tf.keras.losses.
  BinaryCrossentropy(from_logits=True)
  ```

- **Discriminator Loss**

  The discriminator is receiving the images from both that is training images and generator,so while calculating `discriminator_loss` we have to add loss due to real images and also due to fake images both networks are trained simultaneously, so we need two optimizers for both generator and discriminator both. We want from discriminator to output the probabilities close to 1 if the images are real and close to 0 if the images are fake.

  ```
  # ### Discriminator loss

  # This method quantifies how well the discriminator
  is able to distinguish real images from fakes.

  # It compares the discriminator's predictions on
  real images to an array of 1s,

  # and the discriminator predictions on fake
  (generated) images to an array of 0s.

  def discriminator_loss(real_output, fake_output):

  real_loss = cross_entropy(tf.ones_like(real_output),
  real_output)

  fake_loss = cross_entropy(tf.zeros_like(fake_
  output), fake_output)

  total_loss = real_loss + fake_loss

      return total_loss
  ```

- **Generator Loss**

  In case of a generator, we want it to generate such fake images so that it being recognised as a real image by a generator is maximally possible. So we pair fake outputs with one so as to fool the discriminator.

  ```
  ### Generator loss
  ```

  ```
  # The generator's loss quantifies how well it was
  able to trick the discriminator.
  ```

  ```
  # Intuitively, if the generator is performing well,
  the discriminator will classify the fake images as
  real (or 1).
  ```

  ```
  # Here, we will compare the discriminatory decisions
  on the generated images to an array of 1s.
  ```

  ```
  def generator_loss(fake_output):
      return cross_entropy(tf.ones_like(fake_output),
  fake_output)
  ```

Optimizer

Adam optimizer for both generator and discriminator. The discriminator and the generator optimizers are different since we will train two networks separately.

```
# The discriminator and the generator optimizers are
different since we will train two networks separately.
```

```
generator_optimizer = tf.keras.optimizers.Adam(1e-4)
```

```
discriminator_optimizer = tf.keras.optimizers.Adam(1e-4)
```

Training

We start by iterating over the dataset. The generator is given a random vector as an input which is processed to output an image looking like a face. The discriminator is then shown the real face images as well as the generated images.

```
# ### Save checkpoints
```

```
# This notebook also demonstrates how to save and restore
models,
```

```
# which can be helpful in case a long running training
```

```
task is interrupted.
checkpoint_dir = './training_checkpoints'
checkpoint_prefix = os.path.join(checkpoint_dir, "ckpt")
checkpoint = tf.train.Checkpoint(generator_
optimizer=generator_optimizer,
discriminator_optimizer=discriminator_optimizer,
generator=generator,

discriminator=discriminator)
```

Next, we calculate the generator and the discriminator loss. Then, we calculate the gradients of loss with respect to both the generator and the discriminator variables.

```
EPOCHS = 100
noise_dim = 100
num_examples_to_generate = 16

# We will reuse this seed overtime (so it's easier)
# to visualize progress in the animated GIF)
seed = tf.random.normal([num_examples_to_generate, noise_
dim])

# The training loop begins with generator receiving a
random seed as input.
# That seed is used to produce an image.
# The discriminator is then used to classify real images
(drawn from the training set) and fakes images (produced
by the generator).
# The loss is calculated for each of these models, and
the gradients are used to update the generator and
discriminator.

# Notice the use of `tf.function`
# This annotation causes the function to be "compiled".
@tf.function
def train_step(images):
```

```
noise = tf.random.normal([BATCH_SIZE, noise_dim])

with tf.GradientTape() as gen_tape, tf.GradientTape()
as disc_tape:
generated_images = generator(noise, training=True)

real_output = discriminator(images, training=True)

fake_output = discriminator(generated_images,
training=True)

gen_loss = generator_loss(fake_output)

disc_loss = discriminator_loss(real_output, fake_output)

gradients_of_generator = gen_tape.gradient(gen_loss,
generator.trainable_variables) gradients_of_discriminator
= disc_tape.gradient(disc_loss, discriminator.trainable_
variables)                    generator_optimizer.apply_
gradients(zip(gradients_of_generator,generator.trainable_
variables))

 discriminator_optimizer.apply_gradients(zip(gradients_of_
discriminator, discriminator.trainable_variables))
```

Output

After 50 epochs

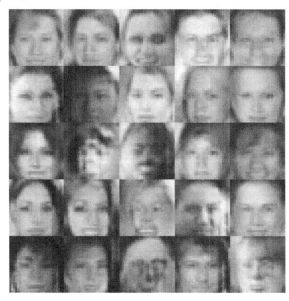

Figure 1.17

We are successful in creating a network in which our generator is finally able to fool discriminator by producing real-like images. Since the generator never had access to real-like image it whatever it outputted was completely different yet similar to our training dataset.

Conclusion

In this chapter, we have focused on learning GAN from a layman's perspective. We have discussed its architecture and explained each component. We also discussed how to build the code for GAN from scratch.

CHAPTER 2
GAN Applications

Introduction

GAN is poised to shake the industry with powerful applications. It has the unimaginable capabilities of denoising images, increasing the quality of images, coloring the grey images, creating new paintings and many more big tasks.

Structure

We shall keep discussing GAN applications for hours and hours. For the sake of clarity and handiness, the chapter discusses vertical-specific GAN applications. For healthcare professionals, it is easy to read all GAN applications for their industry. Similarly, for media and entertainment industry, it is better to focus on their industry-specific GAN applications. Here we have discussed

- Health sector specific GAN applications
- Retail sector-specific GAN applications
- Media and Entertainment sector-specific GAN applications
- Autonomous vehicles sector-specific GAN applications

- Edu Tech sector-specific GAN applications
- Telecom sector-specific GAN applications
- Mixed Reality specific GAN applications

Objective

Help industry professionals know GAN applications in their specific industry

GAN can be used in almost all verticals. Let us start with a simple example. Many times, face images are not complete for some reasons. We can complete the face image through GAN:

Figure 2.1: Image editing is done by GAN

GAN can be applied to various applications. We analyzed some of them on various popular sectors and presented a vertical representation of GAN applications. They are the following:

Health sector-specific GAN applications

GANs can solve the following main challenges in the health sector:

1. Health data generation
2. Medical image segmentation
3. Anomaly detection

Health data generation

Generating multi-label discrete patient records using GAN

Healthcare data is stored in an **electronic health record (EHR)** data. Every healthcare company depends on EHR to make use of data analytics and data science. Due to privacy and compliance issues, EHR data is not easily shared fully or partially. Acquisition of EHR data is a big headache for data scientists and data analysts. Data professionals have to wait for EHR for years and years, mainly due to compliance issues. It also delayed almost all medical research activities. To solve this problem of acquiring meaningful EHR data, GAN can be used to create realistic synthetic data. It is a game-changer in the health industry. Sharing realistic synthetic data has no compliance issues. And that will expedite the data acquisition process and all medical research.

This GAN can be used for:

1. Making colored images of grayscale images for media and movies

2. Making colorful images for old grayscale images

3. Making colorful HD movies from black and white movies

It is a great pleasure to introduce **Medical Generative Adversarial Network (medGAN)** that is used to generate realistic synthetic patient records. Given the real EHR/patient records, medGAN can generate high-dimensional discrete variables via a combination of an autoencoder and generative adversarial networks.

The architecture of medGAN is depicted inthe following figure:

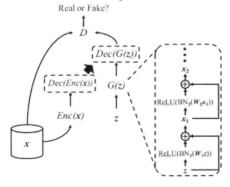

Figure 2.2: Architecture of medGAN

In *figure 2.2*, Architecture of medGAN, the discrete x comes from the source EHR data, z is the random prior for the generator G; G is a feedforward network with shortcut connections (right-hand side figure); an autoencoder (that is, the encoder Enc and decoder Dec) is learned from x; The same decoder Dec is used after the generator G to construct the discrete output. The discriminator D tries to differentiate real input x and discrete synthetic output Dec(G(z)).

MedGAN
Medical image translation using GANs

MedGAN is a complete framework for medical image translation tasks. It combines the conditional adversarial framework with a new combination of non-adversarial losses and a CasNET generator architecture to enhance the global consistency and high-frequency details of results. MedGAN was applied with no task-specific modifications on three challenging tasks in medical imaging: It can be used for:

1. **PET-CTtranslation:** PET Scan to synthetic CT scan

2. **MR motion correction:** Retrospective correction of rigid MR motion artefacts

3. PET denoising

As per many experiments done by medical practitioners, the proposed framework outperformed other similar translation approaches quantitatively and qualitatively across the different proposed tasks.

Generally, two imaging methods provide supplementary information so that two or more types of medical imaging are necessary for a complete diagnostic procedure. One example is hybrid imaging, for example, PET/CT where CT is used for the technical purpose of **attenuation correction (AC)** of PET data. We can get a CT scan synthetically and meaningfully from PET scan if we use this GAN. So, GAN translates/converts PET scan into a synthetic CT scan where the synthetic CT images are not used directly for diagnosis but rather for PET AC. A similar approach was proposed via Cycle-GANs.

Input   Target

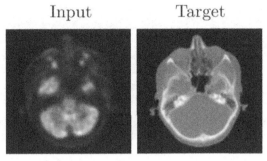

(a) PET-CT translation

Figure 2.3: *Conversion of PET Scan into synthetic CT Scan with GANs*

The correction of rigid and non-rigid motion artefacts in medical images could be viewed as a domain translation problem from motion-corrupted images into motion-free images:

Input   Target

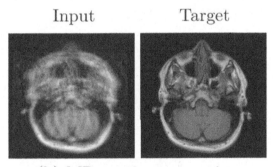

(b) MR motion correction

Figure 2.4: *MR motion Correction with GANs*

Pix2pix GANs were also utilized for the task of denoising low dose CT images by translating it into a high dose counterpart:

Input   Target

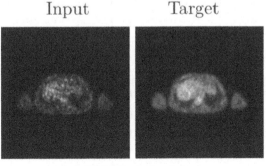

(c) PET denoising

Figure 2.5

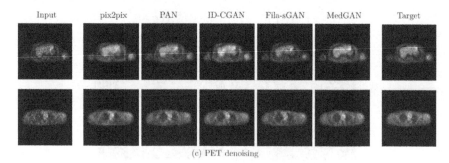

(c) PET denoising

Figure 2.6: Denoising with various types of GANs

The performance of **MedGAN** was compared against several state-of-the-art translation frameworks, including **pix2pix, PAN, IDCGAN,** and **Fila-sGAN**.

MedGANarchitecture

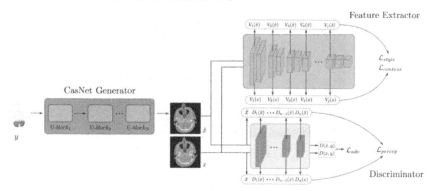

Figure 2.7: MedGANarchitecture

In this MedGAN, this new generator architecture, named as **CasNet**, is inspired by ResNets. It chains together several fully convolutional encoder-decoder networks with skip connections into a single generator network.

Application of MedGAN on three challenging tasks in medical imaging with no application-specific modifications to the hyperparameters. These are a translation from PET images into synthetic CT images, PET image denoising and finally the retrospective correction of rigid MR motion artefacts.

GANs have been gaining more attention in the medical field, especially for image-to-image translation tasks. For instance, a pix2pix architecture with an added gradient-based loss function was utilized for the translation from MR to CT images.

Classically, these medical imaging tasks can be managed through GAN models such aspix2pix, PAN, ID-CGAN and Fila-SGAN models. Let us go deep into each GAN model.

pix2pix

In 2016, pix2pix GAN framework was introduced as a general solution to supervised image-to-image translation problems. In this case, the generator receives as input an image from the input domain (for example, a grayscale photo) and is tasked to translate it to the target domain (for example, a colored photo) by minimizing a pixel-reconstruction error (L1 loss) as well as the adversarial loss. On the other hand, the discriminator is tasked to differentiate between the fake output of the generator and the desired ground truth output image.

pix2pix can be used for the image to image translation, such as:

- Image to segmented images or vice versa
- Aerial photo to map or vice versa
- Grayscale image to color photos.
- Edges to photo.
- Sketch to photo

PAN

In Apr 2019, **Perceptual Adversarial Networks (PAN)** were introduced: It is also aimed at the image to image translation. PAN combines the generative adversarial loss and the proposed perceptual adversarial loss as a novel training loss function:

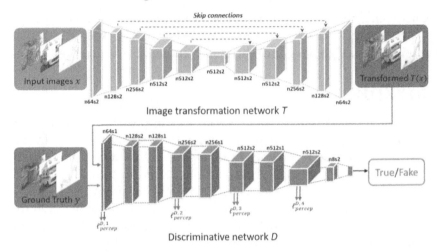

Figure 2.8: PAN

ID-CGAN

Image De-raining Conditional Generative Adversarial Network (ID-CGAN) was introduced in June 2019. It is used for the image to image translation:

Input   De-rained results

Figure 2.9: Results with ID-CGAN

ID-CGAN architecture

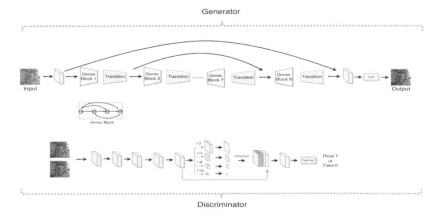

Figure 2.10: ID-CGAN Architecture

Fila-SGAN

Filamentary structured images with GAN is introduced in 2017 to synthesize filamentary structured images given a ground-truth input. The synthesized images are close to reality and have been shown to boost image segmentation performance when used as additional training images. It aims at synthesizing filamentary structured images such as retinal fundus images and neuronal images:

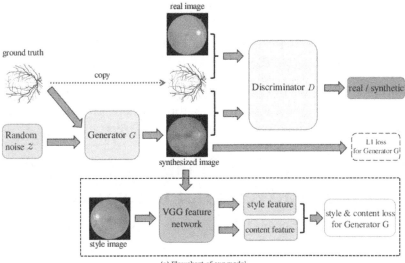

(a) Flowchart of our model

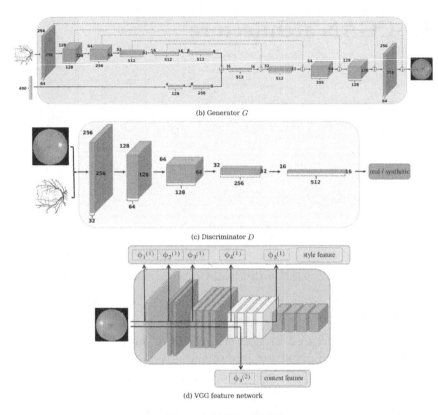

(b) Generator G

(c) Discriminator D

(d) VGG feature network

Figure 2.11: *Fila-SGAN*

Generally, two imaging methods provide supplementary information so that two or more types of medical imaging are necessary for a complete diagnostic procedure. One example is hybrid imaging, for example, PET/CT where CT is used for the technical purpose of AC of PET data. We can get a CT scan synthetically and meaningfully from PET scan if we use this GAN. So, GAN translates/converts PET scan into a synthetic CT scan where the synthetic CT images are not used directly for diagnosis but rather for PET AC.

Synthetic medical images from dual generative adversarial networks

It aims at converting the MRI scan into the CT scan. It happens in two stages

1. Segmentation-mask-generating DCGAN
2. Image-to-image translator using pix2pix

Why do we need?

Answer: **Positron Emission Tomography(PET)/Computed Tomography (CT)** is the X-ray technology-based medical imaging method to generate images of patients based on a technique related to medical isotopes which are given to patients. CT scans are mostly used in diagnosing oncology, serious injuries to the head, chest, spine and pelvis, especially fractures. CT scans are also used to pinpoint the size and location of tumors.

On the other hand, MRI is the magnetic field and radio wave-based medical imaging method. Mostly, a CT scan can often be done in 3-5 minutes while MRIs take around 30 minutes. MRIs is better to diagnose issues in soft tissues,ligaments, and tendons.

As getting a CT scan is a bit risky due to radiation in CT scan process, it is desired to get (synthetic) CT scan directly from MRI images.

CT scan can be translated/converted from MRI Scan using GAN in two stages.

Input: (MRI scan)

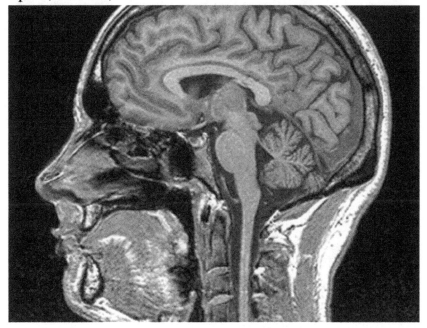

Figure 2.12: Input MRI scan

Output: (CT Scan)

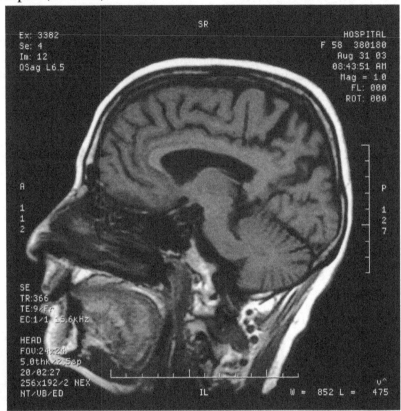

Figure 2.13: Output MRI scan

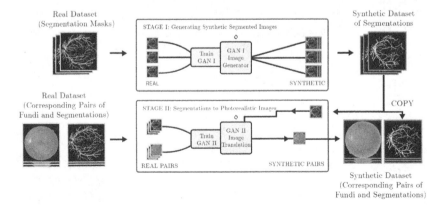

Figure 2.14: Stage GANs showing how the synthetic images are generated as described

Here we have solved the challenge in two stages. In the first stage, the aim is to produce segmentation masks that can take care of geometries of the image. In the second stage, the aim is to enhance the image to make it photorealistic image. So, Stage-II GAN is used to only generate the colors, lighting, and textures of the medical image from the given geometry.

seGAN - medical image segmentation

It is the process of automatic or semi-automatic detection of boundaries within a 2D or 3D medical image. A major difficulty of medical image segmentation is the high variability in medical images.

Input

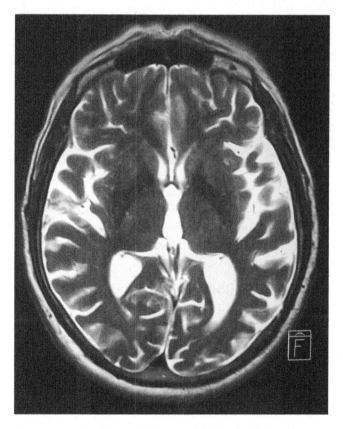

Figure 2.15: Input for seGAN

Output

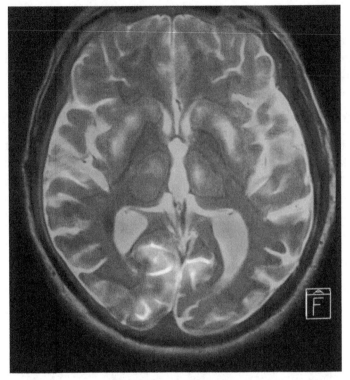

Figure 2.16: Output for seGAN

Medical professionals need to identify the semantically similar zones and tumors for that they need to segment the image into meaningful zones. Even tumor identification and its size calculation aredone after this segmentation task.

As a GAN framework, the segmenter and discriminator networks are trained in an alternating fashion in a min-max game. It requires pixel-level labelling, the single scalar real/fake output of a classic GAN's discriminator may not be effective in producing stable and sufficient gradient feedback to the networks. Instead, we can use a fully convolutional neural network as the segmenter to generate segmentation label maps, and propose a novel adversarial critic network with a multi-scale L1 loss function to force the critic and segmenter to learn both global and local features that capture long- and short-range spatial relationships between pixels.

Masked images are calculated by pixel-wise multiplication of a label map and (the multiple channels of) an input image. Note that, although only one label map (for whole tumor segmentation) is illustrated here, multiple label maps (for examples. also for tumor core and Gd-enhanced tumor core) can be generated by the segmenter in one path.

And eventually, the segmenter will be able to produce predicted label maps that are very close to the ground truth as labelled by human experts.

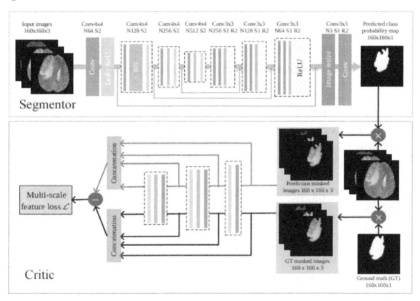

Figure 2.17: Architecture of segAN

segAN results are shown, that represents segmentation of tumor on the human brain.

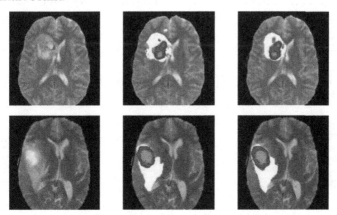

Figure 2.18: segAN results in tumor segmentation on the human brain

Anomaly detection

It is very difficult to identify anomaly image in the image dataset. Suppose you have 10,000 retina images and it is possible that 10-20 retina images have something unusual such as retinal fluids ofhyperreflective foci. It takes huge efforts to identify the anomalous images.

Generative adversarial training is done on healthy data, and testing is performed on both, unseen healthy cases and anomalous data.

Obtaining models that capture imaging markers relevant for disease progression and treatment monitoring is challenging.

Issues with old methods of anomaly detection: Traditionally, models are based on large amounts of data with annotated examples of known markers aiming at automating detection. High annotation effort and the limitation to a vocabulary of known markers limit the power of such approaches.

Here, we can perform unsupervised learning to identify anomalies in imaging data as candidates for markers.

AnoGAN can be used for:

- Identification of anomalous medical images
- Identification of varieties of anomaly pattern in images
- Building anomaly predictor for images
- Anomaly prediction on unannotated images

AnoGAN, a deep convolutional GAN is meant to learn a manifold of normal anatomical variability, it contains a new anomaly scoring scheme based on the mapping from image space to a latent space. Applied to new data, the model labels anomalies, and scores image patches indicating their fit into the learned distribution

The following figure represents the overview of AnoGAN for anomaly detection:

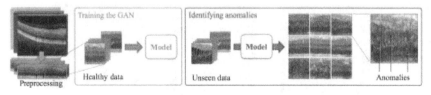

Figure 2.19: Overview of AnoGAN for anomaly detection

Results of AnoGAN is shown in the following figure:

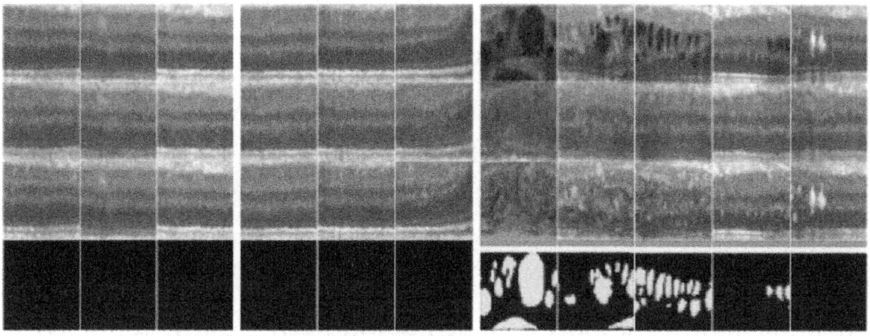

Figure 2.20: Results of AnoGAN

We can see Pixel-level identification of anomalies on exemplary images:

- **First row:** Real input images of the retinal area.
- **Second row:** Proposed mapping approach based corresponding images generated by the model.
- **Third row:** Residual overlay. Redness represents the residual score to identify anomalies. Yellowness describes the discrimination score to identify anomalies.
- **Fourth row:** Pixel-level annotations of retinal fluid.

There are three blocks separated by vertical gaps:

- **First block:** Normal images extracted from OCT volumes of healthy cases in the training set.
- **Second block:** Normal images extracted from OCT volumes of healthy cases in the test set.
- **Third block:** Images extracted from diseased cases in the test set.

Retail sector-specific GAN applications

As financial institutions monitor billions of transactions a day, the data mined from each creates a silo of information and data that any person would find overwhelming to sift through. If intelligently analyzed, these vast stores of data can prove invaluable to these institutions by helping them uncover financial crimes risk. Anti-money laundering (AML) pattern detection helps intelligent systems zero in on anomalies in transaction patterns that might point to money laundering activity. For this, we can use AnoGAN, which is described in the preceding section.

GAN can also be used for enhancing the shopping experience of the user. Where a user who wants to buy Hat, can eventually see how it looks without even trying.

SRGAN

Creating high-resolution images for low-resolution is the need for e-commerce. There are many small dealers and manufacturers, and they may not have good quality images. E-commerce platform companies need to make high-quality images through SRGAN.

Input: Low-resolution image

Figure 2.21: Input for SRGAN(Low Resolution)

Output: High-resolution image

Figure 2.22: Output for SRGAN(High Resolution)

Virtual try-on clothes

GAN model can be built to have virtual try-on. Some startups, such as WoWExp are working on it.

Figure 2.23: Image showing virtual try-on

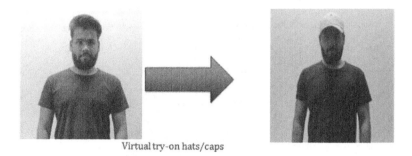

Virtual try-on hats/caps

Figure 2.24: Image showing adding characteristic features

Denoising images

Figure 2.25: Example showing denoising

Sketch to (colorful/realistic)handbag/shoes

Figure 2.26: Showing input back and white image

Figure 2.27: Showing output colorful image

Pose guided person image generation

We mostly need the same person in different poses. We generally take a photo of apparel with one model in one pose. Customers of e-commerce would like to see different pose/perspective. For that, GAN can be used:

Figure 2.28: Showing input image for pose change

GAN can give new pose/perspective. It will give a better experience for e-commerce customers as a single image may not be enough to build confidence.

Figure 2.29: Showing Output image 1 after pose change

PixelDTGAN- taking clothes from celebrity pictures

Many people want to buy what celebrity or their favourite person wear. GAN can be used to take clothes from person-images smartly. E-commerce can use this GAN to help customers buy those dresses, and it can give a lot of revenues.

Input

Figure 2.30: Showing input for PixelDTGA

Output

Figure 2.31: Showing output sweater extracted after PixelDTGAN

A source image.   Possible target images.

Figure 2.32: Showing input and possible outputs extracted after PixelDTGAN

Suggesting merchandise based on celebrity pictures has been popular for fashion blogger and e-commerce. PixelDTGAN creates clothing images and styles from an image:

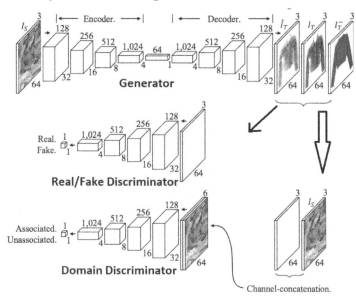

Figure 2.33: Architecture of PixelDTGAN

Disco GAN

It is a very creative idea to do cross-domain work. GAN does it nicely, which can be helpful in offering great new products to customers.

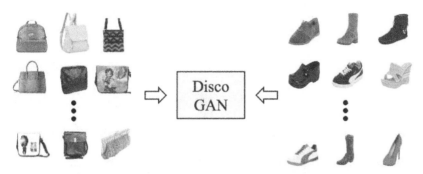

(a) Learning cross-domain relations **without any extra label**

(b) Handbag images (input) & **Generated** shoe images (output)

(c) Shoe images (input) & **Generated** handbag images (output)

Figure 2.34: Input and output of DiscoGAN

It learns how to discover relations between different domains and make cross-domain new images, And that is how this network successfully transfers style from one domain to another without disturbing key attributes such as orientation and face identity.

The architecture of Disco GAN is shown in the following figure:

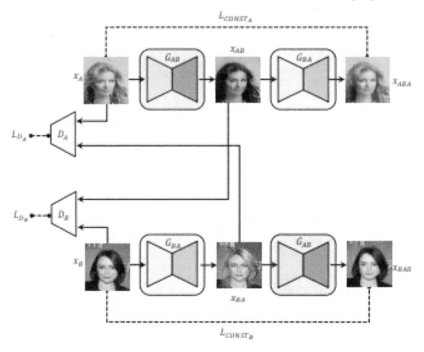

Figure 2.35: Architecture of DiscoGAN

pix2pix - removing the filter from face

pix2pix is discussed in detail in health topics. It can be used to remove the filter from the face:

Input

Output

Ground Truth

Figure 2.36: Input and Output of pix2pix showing how the filter is removed from office

Media and entertainment sector-specific GAN applications

SRGAN

Although we have achieved decent accuracy in super-resolution of images using various approaches in deep learning, we could not get very fine texture details in super-resolution. SRGAN is very powerful to makethe super-resolution with very fine details. It is able to achieve great output even with 4x upscaling factors.

Here is the low-quality image:

Figure 2.37: Low-quality input of SRGAN

If you apply SRGAN, you can get a high-quality image (super-resolution). Here is the output of SRGAN and that is what we need in industry.

Figure 2.38: High-quality output of SRGAN

SRGAN can be used for:

- Making super-resolution of all brand images for media
- Making super-resolution of images taken from a normal camera or phone
- Making high-quality HD movie from a low-quality movie
- Making high-quality footage for news reporting
- Converting old low-resolution images into high-resolution images
- Presenting HD content to customers
- Making a new version/high-resolution version of classical movies

How SRGAN works: It is governed by a perceptual loss function which consists of an adversarial loss and a content loss. The adversarial loss, focused on pixel space similarity, pushes our solution to the natural image manifold using a discriminator network that is trained to differentiate between the super-resolved images and original photo-realistic images. On the other hand, we can use a content loss motivated by perceptual similarity. Here deep residual network is able to recover photo-realistic textures from heavily downsampled images.

The architecture of SRGAN is presented in the following figure:

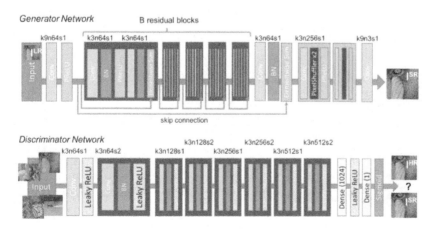

Figure 2.39: SRGAN Architecture

The result of SRGAN is shown in the following figure:

SRResNet	SRGAN-MSE	SRGAN-VGG22	SRGAN-VGG54	original HR image

Figure 2.40: *Different SRGAN implementation with corresponding results*

DeOldify

It aims at converting Old Black and White Movie into Colored Movie

All of us have seen old movies that are black and white movies. Imagine an angel comes to you and you ask for making your old movies color movies.Suppose you see a documentary on World War II, and you wish to see colored version which is almost impossible.

Here comes DeOldify GAN model which converts grayscale image/ video into colored image/video.

Input:

Figure 2.41: *Black and white input of DeOldifyGAN*

Output:

Figure 2.42: Colorfuloutput of DeOldifyGAN

GAN has two deep learning models:

- Generator
- Discriminator

The generator of this GAN is a U-Net. U-Net has basically two halves:

1. One that does visual recognition.
2. The other that outputs an image based on the visual recognition features.

In this case, the U-Net is a Resnet34 pre-trained on ImageNet. Its first half aims at getting features through a pre-trained model. The other half of this generator aims to assign the relevant color based on the object in the image, driven by feature extraction. So, it creates colored images for grayscale images. The output of the generator may not be great in initial iterations. Here comes the role of discriminator/critic that finds the loss and helps in the result improvement process.

This GAN can be used for

1. Making colored images of grayscale images for media and movies
2. Making colorful images for old grayscale images
3. Making colorful HD movies from black and white movies
4. Making colorful footage for old news reporting

5. Making a new version/colorful version of historical records

To make it better, we add the new **attention** layer in both the discriminator and the generator and the spectral normalization. We can use their hinge loss and different learning rates for critic versus generator. But this really made the training a lot more stable. Additionally, the attention layers really made a big difference in terms of consistency of coloration, and general quality.

Self Attention GAN architecture and results are explained in *Figure 2.43* and *Figure 2.44*, respectively:

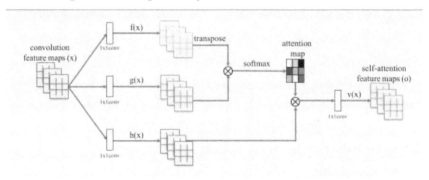

Figure 2.43: Self-attention GAN

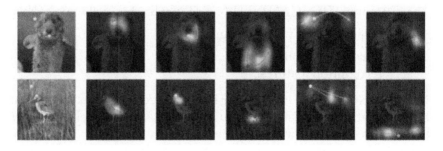

Figure 2.44: Result of self-attention GAN

Stack GAN

Can you imagine an angel who can generate an image if you tell something?

Please start imagining it as it is happening now due to StackGAN. **Stacked Generative Adversarial Networks (StackGAN)** is used to generate 256×256 photo-realistic images if we give a text as an input.

Input: A text

A dog is white with black and is sitting next to a boy

Output: An image

Figure 2.45: Output image of StackGAN

StackGAN can be used for:

1. Converting a comment into an image on social media
2. Converting a fact into a meaningful image
3. Making a document more exciting by adding relevant images
4. Making a great image and video based on the novel
5. Making an email exchange more exciting
6. Making a news report very exciting by adding photos

It breaks the hard problem into subproblems through a sketch-refinement process. It works in two stages:

1. **The Stage-I GAN** aims at getting the primitive shape and colors of the object based on the given text description, and it outputs the low-resolution image. The Stage-II GAN aims at generating high-resolution images with photo-realistic details by using the low-resolution image and text descriptions as inputs.

2. **The Stage II GAN** aims at working on defects in Stage-I results and add finer details and hence Stage II can be considered as refinement stage. To improve the quality of outputs, we introduce a novel conditioning augmentation technique that encourages smoothness in the latent conditioning manifold.

The architecture of stackGAN is following:

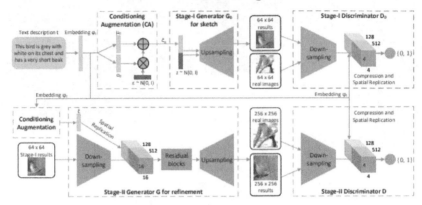

Figure 2.46: Black and white input of DeOldifyGAN

Outputs of stackGAN are the following:

Figure 2.47: Output of Stack-GAN

Face ageing - Age-cGAN

Many social media companies and entertainment companies would like to see how celebrities or any person would look at a very old age. Social media can offer many apps regarding the age change, and this GAN can be useful for that:

Face Aging

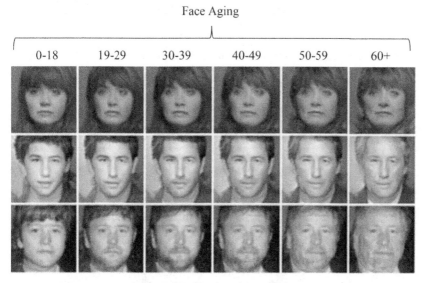

Figure 2.48: Output of Age-cGAN

It can be used for:

- Offering the capability to everyone for getting new looks in various age-group
- Modifying the movie if required
- Making a movie without costume change for actors

GAN architecture can be seen in the following:

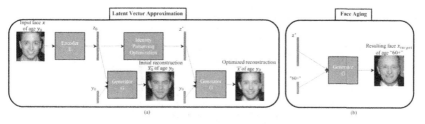

Figure 2.49: Architecture Of Age-cGAN

Domain Transfer Networks (DTN)

We can create emoji from pictures.These emoji are personalized emoji, and it can be used for social media, entertainment and retail:

Figure 4: Shown, side by side are sample images from the CelebA dataset, the emoji images created manually using a web interface (for validation only), and the result of the unsupervised DTN. See Tab. 4 for retrieval performance.

Fig 2.50: Faces from CelebA dataset and their corresponding emoji's

DTN architecture

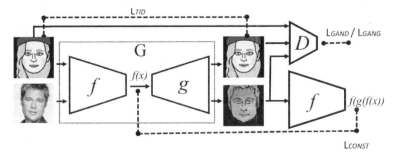

Figure 1: The Domain Transfer Network. Losses are drawn with dashed lines, input/output with solid lines. After training, the forward model G is used for the sample transfer.

Figure 2.51: Architecture of DTN

Autonomous vehicles sector-specific GAN applications

Autonomous vehicles highly depend on the quality of visual information received from the environment. SRGAN can be applied here to enhance the visual quality, that was described in the preceding section.

Autonomous driving testing system

There are many domains where some errors can be tolerated. But, this domain needsa superb level of accuracy; otherwise, it can cause fatal accidents and deaths. Deep neural networks have helped us build some fundamentals of autonomous vehicles. We need huge datasets for training such a complicated model. For that, we need to generate a dataset, and it is a very difficult process to get real data. To solve this issue, we need to generate a realistic synthetic dataset that can look very authentic and contain semantic information of driving scenes. This kind of realistic synthetic data can help us create a reliable and accurate model for autonomous vehicles.

GAN based an unsupervised framework to generate large amounts of synthetic but accurate driving scenes is introduced and known as DeepRoad.In particular, **DeepRoad** delivers driving scenes with various weather conditions (including those with rather extreme conditions) by applying the **Generative Adversarial Networks (GANs)** along with the corresponding real-world weather scenes.

Moreover, we have implemented DeepRoad to test three well-recognized DNN-based autonomous driving systems.

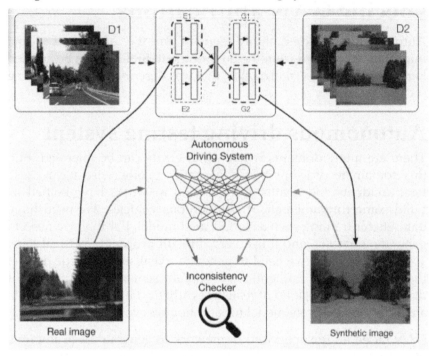

Figure 2.52: DeepRoad Framework

GAN results for environment creation for vehicle testing is represented in the following image:

Figure 2.53: Environment creation by GAN, 1st row represents the actual image and 2nd row repres ents GAN generated image

We need to segment road scene, and that can be done by many kinds of GAN models such as pix2pix, PAN, ID-CGAN, Fila SGAN. We discussed all these approaches tohealthcare topics.

EduTechsector-specific GAN applications

GAN can be used for educational content creation. We can generate video where Albert Einstein teaches his famous theory of relativity. It is one of the applications of pix2pix GAN, which was described in the Health sector-specific GAN *applications* section.

pix2pix

It is discussed in detail in the *Health sector-specific GAN applications* section:

Figure 2.54: example usage of pix2pix

pix2pix is extremely useful for kids' learning processes. It is discussed in detail in health topic. Please see there.

For kids' learning, pix2pix can be used for:

- Converting sketch to photo
- Converting edge to photo
- Daylight scene to night scene

- Black and white image to color image
- Map to aerial images and vice versa

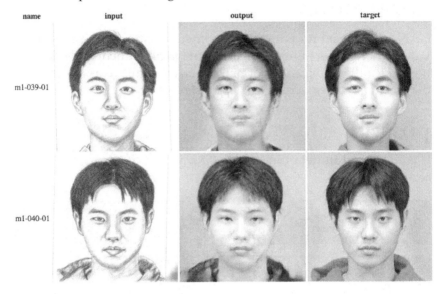

Figure 2.55: Example of pix2pix application

For kids:

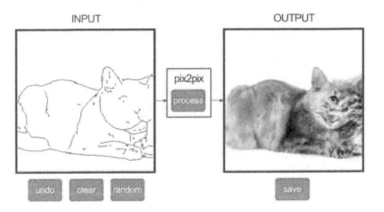

Figure 2.56

SRGAN

It can be used for improving low-quality images/videos to high-quality images/videos. It is discussed in the initial sections.

Denoising GAN

It can be used to correct images.

Image editing - IcGAN

Suppose you want to see your friend in a new look, you can try this ICGAN.

Any face can be modified with heavy makeup, eyeglasses, blonde, black hair, smiling, pale skin:

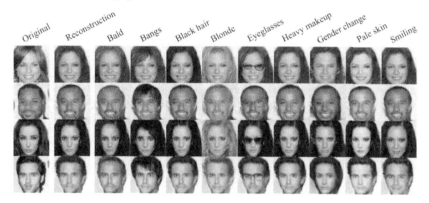

Figure 2.57: Image editing is done with IcGAN

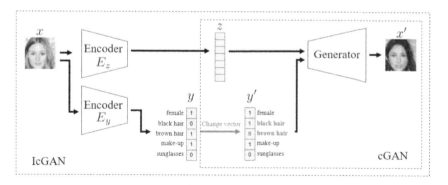

Figure 2.58: Architecture Of IcGAN

Telecom sector-specific GAN applications

In all imaging tasks, we can use pix2pix, PAN and other models.

WaveNet

Creating a realistic synthetic audio dataset is very useful for automating customer care and for creating creative tones. Suppose you want to know audio of your father saying something unusual words. Suppose telecom companies want to offer a personalized tune to their customers, they can create using WaveNet.

This GAN can create synthetic audi dataset of birds, humans, animals.

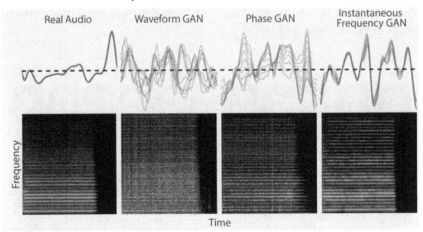

Figure 2.59: Output Of Audio output generated from different types of GAN

The WaveGAN and PhaseGAN, however, have many phase irregularities, creating a blurry web of lines. The IFGAN is much more coherent, having only small variations from cycle-to-cycle. In the Rainbowgrams below, the real data and IF models have coherent waveforms that result in strong, consistent colors for each harmonic, while the PhaseGAN has many speckles due to phase discontinuities, and the WaveGAN model is quite irregular.

GANSynth

GANSynth uses a progressive GAN architecture to incrementally upsample with convolution from a single vector to the full sound.

It works mostly for highly periodic sounds, like those found in music

Mixed reality specific GAN applications

Mixed reality needs 3D objects for a better immersive experience. We need to convert 2D images into 3D images. Suppose you are given a photo, you want to see in 3D view. It is almost impossible.

Thanks to GAN that makes it possible, especially for regular items.

3D-GAN generates 3D objects from 2D images. Results have been astonishing.

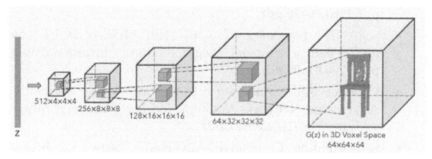

Figure 2.60: Generator Architecture of 3D-GAN

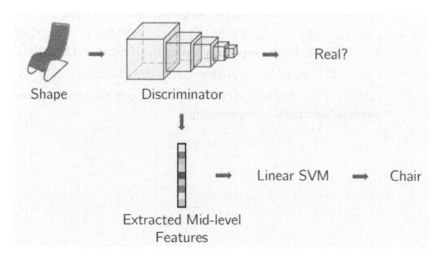

Figure 2.61: Discriminator Architecture of 3D-GAN

Conclusion

It is an immense pleasure to introduce GAN and its powerful applications to every industry. I hope you will get new ideas after reading this chapter.

References

- Generating Multi-label Discrete Patient Records using Generative Adversarial Networks: **https://arxiv.org/pdf/1703.06490.pdf**
- SegAN: Adversarial Network with Multi-scale L1 Loss for Medical Image Segmentation: **https://arxiv.org/pdf/1706.01805.pdf**
- Unsupervised Anomaly Detection with Generative Adversarial Networks to Guide Marker Discovery: **https://arxiv.org/pdf/1703.05921.pdf**
- Self-Attention Generative Adversarial Networks: **https://arxiv.org/pdf/1805.08318.pdf**
- DeepRoad: GAN-based Metamorphic Autonomous Driving System Testing: **https://arxiv.org/pdf/1802.02295.pdf**
- GANSYNTH: ADVERSARIAL NEURAL AUDIO SYNTHESIS: **https://openreview.net/pdf?id=H1xQVn09FX**
- Disco GAN:https://arxiv.org/pdf/1703.05192.pdf
- Github for many GANs: **https://github.com/tensorflow/models/tree/master/research/gan**

CHAPTER 3
Problem with GAN

Introduction

GAN has proven great results in many generative responsibilities to duplicate the actual-global rich content material, including images, human language, and track. It is stimulated by way of game theory: two models, a generator and a discriminator are competing with every different whilst making each other stronger at the same time. But, it's challenging to train GANs for many reasons including instability, failure to converge, high computation cost, poor quality of the result. We shall discuss the main feature of GAN such as KL divergence, JS divergence, Nash equilibrium in this chapter.

This chapter aims at understanding challenges. For that, we need to understand the nitty-gritty of GAN.

First, we shall illustrate KL divergence with discrete and continuous distributions. Then we shall illustrate Nash equilibrium. Then we shall discuss the improvement strategies for training GANs.

Sections of this chapter are the following:

- The objective function for training GAN
- KL divergence and JS divergence
  - o KL divergence for discrete probability distributions
  - o KL divergence for continuous probability distributions
- Nash equilibrium
- Mode collapse
- Instability of adverse training
- Weak gradient

The objective function for training GAN

As we know that GAN is inspired by the zero-sum non-cooperative game. This is also called a **minimax game**, where one network (the discriminator) wants to maximize the objective function (the chance of the generated images to be called right). In-game theory, the GAN model converges when the discriminator (player A) and the generator (Player B) reach a Nash equilibrium. This is the optimal point for the minimax equation.

Training GAN is equivalent to minimizing JS divergence (or KL divergence) between probability distribution q (estimated distribution, from the generator)and probability distribution p (the real-life distribution). In layman's words, JS divergence (or KL divergence) represents the distance between two probability distribution functions. We shall explore KL divergence and JS divergence and then discuss its pros and cons.

KL divergence

- **Kullback–Leibler (KL)** divergence: It measures how one probability distribution p diverges from a second expected probability distribution q.

$$D_{KL}(p\|q) = \int_x p(x) \log \frac{p(x)}{q(x)} dx$$

Figure 3.1

Jensen–Shannon divergence: JS divergence is symmetric and smoother.

$$D_{JS}(p\|q) = \frac{1}{2}D_{KL}(p\|\frac{p+q}{2}) + \frac{1}{2}D_{KL}(q\|\frac{p+q}{2})$$

Figure 3.2

In layman words, JS divergence can be considered a better version of KL divergence. If we understand KL divergence, we get the idea of JS divergence.

KL Divergence is meant to measure the distance between the probability distributions.KL Divergence between two probability distributions is to be measured.

Probability distributions can be discrete or continuous.

First, let us explore KL divergence between two discrete probability distributions.

KL divergence between two discrete probability distributions

Non-symmetric difference between two probability distributions, defined over some type of outcomes.

You have two dice A and B.

Die A and Die B have different probability distributions, having outcomes 1, 2, 3, 4, 5, 6.

Ideally, the die has an equal chance of each outcome, but in reality, die has an unequal chance of each outcome. Based on experience with a die/dice, we can come to know the probability distributions of a die. Here we consider two dice A and B.

Chance of 1, 2, 3 ,4 ,5, 6 in Die A is:

$$p(a_1) = \frac{1}{12}, p(a_2) = \frac{1}{12}, p(a_3) = \frac{1}{12}, p(a_4) = \frac{1}{6}, p(a_5) = \frac{1}{3}, p(a_6) = \frac{1}{4}$$

Figure 3.3

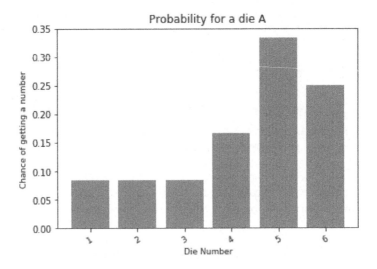

Figure 3.4: *Graph showing the number on the die A and the chance of getting that number*

That of Die B is:

$$p(b_1) = \frac{1}{12}, p(b_2) = \frac{1}{12}, p(b_3) = \frac{1}{12}, p(b_4) = \frac{1}{6}, p(b_5) = \frac{1}{4}, p(b_6) = \frac{1}{3}$$

Figure 3.5

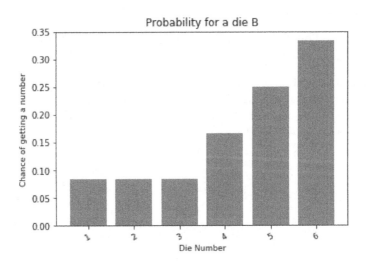

Figure 3.6: *Graph showing the number on the die B and the chance of getting that number*

KL divergence, the difference between two probability distributions of Die A and Die B

$$KL\ (A||B) = \sum_{i=1}^{n} p(a_i)\ ln\ ln\ \frac{p(a_i)}{p(b_i)}$$

Here$KL\ (A||B) = \frac{1}{12}\ ln\ ln\ \left(\frac{1/12}{1/12}\right) + \frac{1}{12}\ ln\ ln\ \left(\frac{1/12}{1/12}\right) + \frac{1}{12}\ ln\ ln\ \left(\frac{1/12}{1/12}\right) + \frac{1}{6}\ ln\ ln\ \left(\frac{1/6}{1/6}\right) + \frac{1}{3}\ ln\ ln\ \left(\frac{1/3}{1/4}\right) + \frac{1}{4}\ ln\ ln\ \left(\frac{1/4}{1/3}\right)$

$$= 0 + 0 + 0 + 0 + 0 + \frac{1}{3}\ ln\ \frac{4}{3} + \frac{1}{4}\ ln\ \frac{3}{4}$$

$$= 0.024$$

KL (A//B) ≠KL (B//A) in general.

Suppose you have three Dice A, B, and C.

You can quantify the non-symmetric difference between die A and die B and that between dice A and dice C.

$$KL\ (A||B) > KL\ (A||C)$$

Then A is more similar to C than to B.

(In layman words, KL means the distance between distributions.)

KL Divergence between two continuous probability distributions

Here you can see distribution A (blue color):

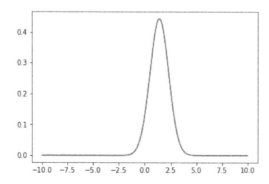

Figure 3.7: *Distribution A*

See distribution **A** (blue color) and distribution **B** (green color):

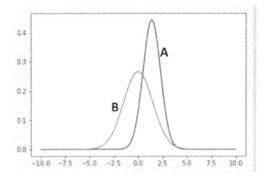

Figure 3.8: Distribution A and B

See distribution **A** (blue color) and distribution **C** (red color):

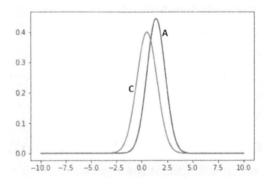

Figure 3.9: Distribution A and C

Can you tell which distribution (**B** or **C**) is more close to distribution **A**?

We have tried to find the similarity (or distance) between the distributions:

- **Distance between distributions A and B:** 2.6095910558647555
- **Distance between distributions A and C:** 0.7226444662751103

Here KL divergence comes to the rescue.

KL divergence is an important measure of how one probability distribution diverges from a secondprobability distribution. So, if the value of divergence is really small, then they are very close. If the number is high, then they are far apart.

Let us see the mathematics of two continuous probability distributions. For simplicity, we can take Gaussian distributions.

For continuous probability distributions, KL divergence can be expressed as:

$$KL\,(q||p) = \int q(x)\ln\frac{q(x)}{p(x)}$$

Take an example of gaussian distributions:

$$p(x) = \frac{1}{\sqrt{2\pi\sigma^2}}\exp\left(-\frac{(x-\mu)^2}{2\sigma^2}\right) = N\,(x|\mu,\sigma^2)$$

$$q(x) = \frac{1}{\sqrt{2\pi s^2}}\exp\left(-\frac{(x-m)^2}{2s^2}\right) = N\,(x|m,s^2)$$

Now $\ln\left(\frac{q(x)}{p(x)}\right) = \ln\frac{x}{\sigma} + \left[\frac{(x-\mu)^2}{2\sigma^2} - \frac{(x-m)^2}{2s^2}\right]$

$$= \ln\frac{\sigma}{s} + \left(\frac{1}{2\sigma^2} - \frac{1}{2s^2}\right)x^2 - \left(\frac{\mu}{\sigma^2} - \frac{m}{s^2}\right)x + \left(\frac{\mu^2}{2\sigma^2} - \frac{m}{2s^2}\right)$$

$$KL\,(q||p) = q(x)\ln\left(\frac{q(x)}{p(x)}\right)$$

$$= \left(\frac{\sigma}{s}\right)\int xN\,(x|\,m,s^2)dx + \left(\frac{1}{2\sigma^2} - \frac{1}{2s^2}\right)\int x^2\,N\,(x|\,m,s^2)dx + \left(\frac{\mu^2}{2\sigma^2} - \frac{m^2}{2s^2}\right)\int N\,(x|\,m,s^2)dx$$

:======================================

Note: $\int N\,(x|\,m,s^2)dx = 1$

$$\int xN\,(x|\,m,s^2)dx = m$$

$$\int x^2\,N\,(x|\,m,s^2)dx = m^2 + s^2$$

It is calculus.

Please feel free to try this integration (minus infinite to infinite):

$$\int \frac{1}{\sqrt{2\pi s^2}}\exp\left(-\frac{(x-m)^2}{2s^2}\right)dx$$

It would be equal to 1

And this integration

$$\int x \frac{1}{\sqrt{2\pi s^2}} \exp\left(-\frac{(x-m)^2}{2s^2}\right) dx$$

would be equal to m

And this integration

$$\int x^2 \frac{1}{\sqrt{2\pi s^2}} \exp\left(-\frac{(x-m)^2}{2s^2}\right) dx$$

would be equal to $m^2 + s^2$

===

$$\therefore KL(q||p) = \ln\left(\frac{\sigma}{s}\right) + \left(\frac{1}{2\sigma^2} - \frac{1}{2s^2}\right)(m^2 + s^2) - \left(\frac{\mu}{\sigma^2} - \frac{m}{s^2}\right)m + \left(\frac{\mu^2}{2\sigma^2} - \frac{m^2}{2s^2}\right)$$

After simplification, $KL(q||p) = \ln\left(\frac{\sigma}{s}\right) + \frac{(\mu-m)^2 + s^2}{2\sigma^2} - \frac{1}{2}$

The above equation is valid for measuring KL divergence between two Gaussian probability distributions. Let us focus on special cases:

- **Special case 1:** Two probability distributions whose variance is same that is, σs. Then KL divergence becomes:

$$KL(q||p) = 0 + 0 - \left(\frac{\mu-m}{\sigma^2}\right)m + \left(\frac{\mu^2-m^2}{2\sigma^2}\right)$$

$$\frac{\mu^2 - 2\mu m + m^2}{2\sigma^2} = \frac{(\mu-m)^2}{2\sigma^2}$$

Example: Two probability distribution, $p(x) = N(x | \mu, \sigma^2)$ where $\mu=2$

$q(x) = N(x | m, s^2)$ where $m = 3$ and their variance is same, that is equal to 1

$$KL(q||p) = \frac{(2-3)^2}{2 \times 1} = \frac{1}{2} = 0.5$$

- **Special case 2:** Two probability distributions whose meanis same that is, $\mu = m$ Then KL divergence becomes:

$$KL(q||p) = \ln\left(\frac{\sigma}{s}\right) + \left(\frac{1}{2\sigma^2} - \frac{1}{2s^2}\right)(m^2 + s^2) - \frac{m^2}{2\sigma^2} + \frac{m^2}{2s^2}$$

Example: Two probability distribution, $p(x) = N(x \mid \mu, \sigma^2)$ where variance, $\sigma^2 = 0.25$

$q(x) = N(x \mid m, s^2)$ where variance, $s^2 = 1$ and the mean of each distributionis same, that is equal to 2

Then KL divergence

$$\text{KL}(q \mid\mid p) = \ln\left(\frac{0.5}{1}\right) + \left(\frac{1}{2 \times 0.25} - \frac{1}{2 \times 1}\right)(2{*}2 + 1) - (2{*}2)/(2{*}0.25) + (2{*}2)/(2{*}1)$$

$$= -\ln 2 + (2 - 0.5){*}\ 5 - 8 + 2 = -0.693 + 1.5 = 0.80685$$

Since Kl divergence is low, these probability distributions can be claimed to be similar.

We can see the code for doing the same:

Define the KL_Divergence function to compute the similarity between two Gaussian distributions:

```
def KL_divergence_for_gaussian_distributions(q,p): # q || p
  mu=p[0] #mean of gaussian distribution p
  sig=p[1]  #std. deviation of gaussian distribution p
  m=q[0]  #mean of gaussian distribution q
  s=q[1]  #std. deviation of gaussian distribution p

  return np.log(sig/s) + (((mu-m)**2 + s**2)/(2* (sig**2))) -(1/2)
```

Figure 3.10

Let's define two Gaussian distribution:

```
| # define mean and std. deviation for gaussian distribution
  p=[2, 0.5]
  q=[2 ,1]
```

Figure 3.11

Now, compute KL_divergence:

```
KL_divergence_for_gaussian_distributions(q,p) # q || p
```

```
0.8068528194400546
```

Figure 3.12

So far, you understood how to calculate the KL_divergence between two univariate Gaussian distributions. On the same logic, we find that between multivariate gaussian distributions. In reality, we need to find KL (or JS) divergence between two multivariate Gaussian distribution. So, you can expect huge operations to calculate KL_divergence.

Nash equilibrium

In-Game theory, we see multiplayers playing a game. In a non-cooperative game, players have to take care of their own interest. In every walk of life, including politics, religion, and companies, we can see the game theory. Scientist John Nash suggests that we expect an equilibrium point where each player can not get extra benefit by changing the decision/course. In other words, Nash equilibrium is all about a condition in which every player has optimized its outcome, based on the other players' expected decision. The Nash equilibrium is actually a game theory that states no player can increase his or her payoff by choosing a different action given the other player's actions.

Prisoner's dilemma

The prisoner's dilemma is considered as a standard example of a g ame analyzed in game theory that shows why two completely rational individuals might not cooperate, even if it appears that it is in their best interests to do so. So according to John Nash, the dominant strategy (the strategy for one - no matter what the other person does) is to confess/betrays other. Even though the best possible outcome is actually for both parties to keep quiet.

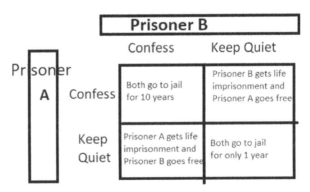

Figure 3.13 Image showing all the possibilities when Prisoner A and Prisoner B confess / keep quiet

(Confess means the one betrays other that is, he/she blames other)

Example

Suppose two employees, Navin and Pramsu, have keys to the office and they are supposed to open the office gate. One morning, they are coordinating about when to reach the office. If Navin reach the office and Pramsu is late, then Navin has to waste time. Same if Pramsu reaches the office and Navin go late, Pramsu wastes time. The Nash equilibrium occurs when both of us reach office early enabling us to spend cool time together or both of us reaching late avoiding discomfort to anyone.

In GAN, adversarial training occurs as one neural network (discriminator) maximizes the function which another neural network tries to minimize. At this equilibrium, each neural network converges on the optimal strategy.

Two models are trained simultaneously to find a Nash equilibrium to a two-player non-cooperative game. However, each model updates its cost independently with no respect foranother player in the game. Updating the gradient of both models concurrently cannot guarantee convergence.

GANs are hard to train. In practice, they do not easily meet Nash equilibrium requirements.

The mentality behind solving GAN training problems

GANs are not a single objective problem so approach which addresses single.

Objective problems fail. No regret algorithms such as gradient descent are guaranteed to converge to coarse correlated equilibria in games. However, the dynamics do not converge for Nash Equilibrium and do not even stabilize in general.

Mode collapse

We know that GAN is a complicated architecture. Mode Collapse is an architectural problem of GAN architecture.

During GAN training, the generator may fail to generate significantly different outputs, that is called **Mode Collapse**. As training is a stochastic process, especially in initial iterations, the generated samples will vary depending on z and the samples were drawn from the real distribution will also vary. In other words, the gradients backpropagated to the generator will vary between training steps depending on the generated and real samples.

In other words, when the generator learns to produce samples that only fit a part of the real distribution. For example, we try to train GAN for generating anew kind of animals. Ideally, we should be expecting a variety of new animals. But, due to unfortunate sampling(based on Z), the generator starts creating almost the same new animal all the time. This issue is called **Mode Collapse**.

The severity of mode collapse may be the complete collapse (all generated samples are almost identical) or partial collapse (most of the samples share significantly common properties).

Moreover, in principle, the discriminator should be able to identify generator mode collapse if it's happening and assign the collapse point a low probability to force the generator to spread out.It is a big reason for the success of GAN training.

Three spaces of GAN training:
1. The space of the real data distribution
2. The classification space of the newly trained critic network
3. The (latent) space based on which the generator generates the image

The idea is to develop a mechanism for the generator to be able to recognize various possible real data modes in addition to trying just to fool the discriminator For this, we add an extra dimension to the latent space of the given dataset, intentionally.

Instability of adversarial training

As we know that GANs are made of two competing neural networks:
- Generator network
- Discriminator network

In initial iterations, both networks don't perform nicely. With each iteration, the generator tries to learn how to fool the discriminator by creating better images, and the discriminator gets better at telling apart the real images from the fakes.

This is called a minimax game, where one network (the discriminator/the critic) wants to maximize the objective function (the chance of the generated images to be called right)

Adversarial training is unstable as it works by training two neural networks, working against each other with the assumed goal that both networks will eventually reach the equilibrium, better known as the **Nash equilibrium**. Although the goal is assumed that both networks would converge, there is no guarantee that competing gradient updates will result in convergence. In practice, it has been seen that adversarial objectives can result in random oscillations of training losses.

Lack of a proper evaluation metric

Generative adversarial networks don't have an excellent objection characteristic which could inform us of the training development. Without a good evaluation metric, it's like running inside the dark. No appropriate signal to tell whilst to prevent; No proper indicator to compare the performance of multiple GAN's.

Vanishing gradient

GAN faces a dilemma:

- If the discriminator behaves badly, the generator does not have accurate feedback, and the loss function cannot represent reality.

- If the discriminator does a great job, the gradient of the loss function drops down to close to zero, and the learning becomes super slow or even jammed.

This dilemma clearly is capable of making the GAN training very tough.

Improving training

One-sided label smoothing

While feeding the discriminator, instead of providing 1 and 0 labels, use floatvalues such as 0.8 and 0.1. It is shown to reduce the networks' vulnerability.

Virtual batch normalization (VBN)

Each data sample is normalized based on a fixed batch (reference batch) of data rather than within its minibatch. The reference batch is chosen once at the beginning and stays the same through the training.

Adding noises

Adding noises is an artificial way tospread out the distribution and to create higher chances for two probability distributions to have overlapped. This is done by adding continuous noises onto the inputs of the discriminator D.

Minibatch discrimination

With minibatch discrimination, the discriminator is able to learnthe relationship between training data points in one batch, instead of processing each point independently.

Use a better metric of distribution similarity

The loss function of the vanilla GAN measures the JS divergence between the distributions of Pr and Pg. This metric fails to provide a meaningful value when two distributions are disjoint. Wasserstein metric is proposed to replace JS divergence because it has a much smoother value space.

Wasserstein GAN (WGAN)

WGAN is an improvised version of GAN , where the training methodology is improvised to make the learning of GANs much more stable and help the model learn more meaningful curves.

Wasserstein distance

Wasserstein Distance is a measure of the distance between two probability distributions. It is also called **Earth Mover's (EM)** distance because informally it can be interpreted as the minimum energy cost of moving and transforming a pile of dirt in the shape of one probability distribution to the shape of the other distribution.

The cost is quantified by the amount of dirt moved x the moving distance.

In a discrete domain, for example, suppose we have two distributions P and Q, each has four piles of dirt and both have ten shovelfuls of dirt in total. The numbers of shovelfuls in each dirt pile are assigned as follows:

$$P_1 = 3, P_2 = 2, P_3 = 1, P_4 = 4$$
$$Q_1 = 1, Q_2 = 2, Q_3 = 4, Q_4 = 3$$

Figure 3.14

In order to change P to look like Q:
- First, move 2 shovelfuls from *P1 to P2* => *(P1,Q1)* match up.
- Then move 2 shovelfuls from *P2 to P3* => *(P2,Q2)* match up.
- Finally, move 1 shovelful from *Q3 to Q4* => *(P3,Q3)* and *(P4, Q4)* match up.

If we label the cost to pay to make Pi and Qi match as δi, we would have:

$$δi + 1 = δi + Pi - Qi$$

$$δ_0 = 0$$
$$δ_1 = 0 + 3 - 1 = 2$$
$$δ_2 = 2 + 2 - 2 = 2$$
$$δ_3 = 2 + 1 - 4 = -1$$
$$δ_4 = -1 + 4 - 3 = 0$$

$$W = \sum |δ_i| = 5.$$

Figure 3.15

Why is Wasserstein better than JS or KL divergence?

Even when two distributions are located in lower-dimensional manifolds without overlaps, Wasserstein distance can still provide a meaningful and smooth representation of the distance in-between.

The WGAN paper exemplified the idea with a simple example.

Suppose we have two probability distributions, P and Q:

$$\forall (x,y) \in P, x = 0 \text{ and } y \sim U(0,1)$$
$$\forall (x,y) \in Q, x = \theta, 0 \leq \theta \leq 1 \text{ and } y \sim U(0,1)$$

Figure 3.16

When $\theta \neq 0$:

$$D_{KL}(P\|Q) = \sum_{x=0, y \sim U(0,1)} 1 \cdot \log \frac{1}{0} = +\infty$$

$$D_{KL}(Q\|P) = \sum_{x=\theta, y \sim U(0,1)} 1 \cdot \log \frac{1}{0} = +\infty$$

$$D_{JS}(P,Q) = \frac{1}{2}\left(\sum_{x=0, y \sim U(0,1)} 1 \cdot \log \frac{1}{1/2} + \sum_{x=0, y \sim U(0,1)} 1 \cdot \log \frac{1}{1/2} \right) = \log 2$$

$$W(P,Q) = |\theta|$$

Figure 3.17

But when $\theta = 0$, two distributions are fully overlapped:

$$D_{KL}(P\|Q) = D_{KL}(Q\|P) = D_{JS}(P,Q) = 0$$
$$W(P,Q) = 0 = |\theta|$$

Figure 3.18

DKL gives us infinity when two dist ributions are disjoint. The value of DJS has a sudden jump, not differentiable at $\theta = 0$. Only the Wasserstein metric provides a smooth measure, which is super helpful for a stable learning process using gradient descents.

Wasserstein distance as GAN loss function

$$W(p_r, p_g) = \frac{1}{K} \sup_{\|f\|_L \leq K} \mathbb{E}_{x \sim p_r}[f(x)] - \mathbb{E}_{x \sim p_g}[f(x)]$$

Figure 3.19

Conclusion

In this chapter, we have gone through the nitty-gritty of GAN. We have discussed the objective function that is KL divergence and JS divergence. We have understood the divergence with the help of many examples in continuous and discrete space. We have also discussed Game Theory that plays akey role in GAN. Limitations and ways to overcome it are also discussed.

CHAPTER 4
Famous Types of GANs

GAN is a recent machine learning technology introduced by *Google Brain Team*. It creates new data instances which look like your training data. In GANs generator and discriminator works in pair. The generator tries to generate target output by learning noisy data, and the generator tries to learn to distinguish true data from the output of the generator. As generator and discriminator have an opposing objective function, which means if one of model changes its behaviour, then so does the other.

Structure

- What is Generative Adversarial Network
- Conditional Generative Adversarial Network
- DC-GAN
- InfoGAN
- Pix2Pix
- PAN
- ID-CGAN
- Stack GAN

- Cycle GAN
- Style GAN
- Radial GAN
- Conclusion
- Exercise

Objective

- Learn the purpose of GAN
- Types of GAN, their architectural model, training, loss function and results
- Coding structure of various GAN models

Generative Adversarial Network

Generative describes a class of statistical models that contrasts with discriminative models.

Generative generate new data instances, discriminative discriminate between different kinds of two data instances.

If we understand it in statistical techniques, if you have data instances X and set of labels Y then,

- Generative models capture the joint probability $P(X,Y)$ or $P(X)$ if there are no labels.
- Discriminative models capture the conditional probability $P(X/Y)$

Following steps are performed in a basic GAN network:

1. Random numbers are fed into the generator and image is generated.
2. The generated image is fed into the discriminator along with other images taken from real datasets.
3. The discriminator considers all of the images fed into it and produce probability as to whether it thinks the image is real or fake.

The discriminator is a standard convolutional network which categorizes image being fed to it. It performs downsampling and classifies the image in a binary fashion.

The generator is conversely reverse of convolution network.The generator takes random noise as input and performs upsampling produce an output image.

Training GAN's

- **Training the generator:** The discriminatorshould be pre-trained against the original datasets.

- **Training the discriminator:** Generator values should be held constant.

Either side of GAN tries to overcome others if one is high performing the other.If discriminator is high performing means it provides output close to 0 or 1, then the generator will have difficulty in reading gradient.If the generator is high performing means it will use the weakness in discriminatory and it will produce false-negative output.

So we will try to stop winning one side of GAN so that both sides can learn together for an extended period of time.

Conditional Generative Adversarial Network (cGAN)

In conditional GAN we are putting some prior condition of extra information y that is fed in both discriminators as well as the generator.So we can understand in generator some noise (z) and y as an input in generator hidden function and in discriminator x(real data) and y is provided in generator hidden function as an input.

Applications

There is a wide-ranging suite of possible applications for cGANs.

- **image-to-image translation:** This technique is used to convert one type of image to others like you have edge image of a bag you will convert it into the real image of the bag after colorization and super-resolution. This led to the development of cGAN-based software, pix2pixHD (images).

- **Text-to-image synthesis:** This technique is used to generate a text description of a given image through GAN - CLS concept.

- **Video generation:** This technique involves a deep neural network that can predict future frames in a natural video sequence.

- **Convolutional face generation:** cGANs use to generate faces with specific attributes from nothing but random noise.

- **Generating shadow maps:** In this technique Scientist introduced an additional sensitivity parameter to the generator that effectively parameterized the loss of the trained detector, proving more efficient than previous state-of-the-art methods.

- **Diversity-sensitive computer vision tasks:** In this technique scientist explicitly regularizes the generator to produce diverse outputs depending on latent codes, with demonstrated effectiveness on three cGAN tasks:

  o image-to-image translation

  o image inpainting

  o video prediction/generation

Architecture

cGAN is a conditional model in which both the generator and discriminator are conditioned on some extra information y.

Example: for MNIST data, condition y, is the label one-hot vector (10-length)

We concatenate this vector y with real x, and then we feed it to the discriminator (D).

```
noise = Input(shape=(self.latent_dim,))
label = Input(shape=(1,), dtype='int32')
label_embedding = Flatten()(Embedding(self.num_classes, self.latent_dim)(label))
model_input = multiply([noise, label_embedding])
```

Figure 4.1

Also, we will concatenate this vector y with noise z, after that is fed it to the generator(G).

```
noise = Input(shape=(100,))
label = Input(shape=(1,))
img = self.generator([noise, label])
```

Figure 4.2

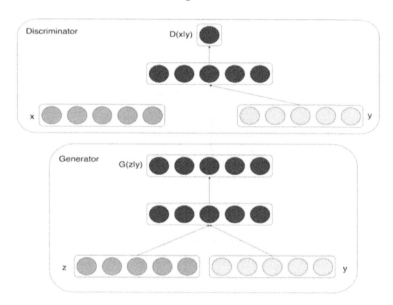

Figure 4.3

Mini-Max condition in cGAN

$$\min_{G} \max_{D} V(D,G) = \mathbb{E}_{x \sim p_{\text{data}}(x)}[\log D(x|y)] + \mathbb{E}_{z \sim p_z(z)}[\log(1 - D(G(z|y)))].$$

Figure 4.4

LOSS

- **Discriminator D, user have info *x* and class *y*:** Orders the information picture is genuine.

- **Generator G, the user provides with noise z, and class y:** Produces the picture which is conditioned by y.

```
# Train the discriminator
d_loss_real = self.discriminator.train_on_batch([imgs, labels], valid)

d_loss_fake = self.discriminator.train_on_batch([gen_imgs, labels], fake)

d_loss = 0.5 * np.add(d_loss_real, d_loss_fake)
```

Figure 4.5

Now loss concept in the generator:

```
# Train the generator
g_loss = self.combined.train_on_batch([noise, sampled_labels], valid)
```

Figure 4.6

$$L_D^{CGAN} = E\big[\log(D(x,c))\big] + E\big[\log(1 - D(G(z),c))\big]$$
$$L_G^{CGAN} = E\big[\log(D(G(z),c))\big]$$

Figure 4.7

Subsequent to preparing, on the off chance that we give a one-hot vector of 3 digits as y and commotion z to the generator G, then the educated generator gives a yield which resembles 3 manually written digits.

DCGAN

A **Deep Convolutional GAN (DCGAN)** accomplishes something fundamentally the same as, yet explicitly focuses on utilizing deep convolutional organizes instead of those completely associated systems.

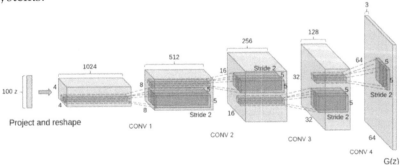

Figure 4.8

ConvNets all in all discover territories of connection inside a picture, that is, they search for spatial relationships. This implies a DCGAN would probably be all the more fitting for picture/video information, though the general thought of a GAN can be connected to more extensive areas, as the model points of interest are left open to be addressed by individual model structures.

In addition, although GAN is known for its difficulty in learning, this paper introduces various techniques for successful learning:

- In GAN as in conventional CNN, we are replacing any pooling layers with stride convolutions (discriminator) and fractional-strided convolutions (generator).

- Batchnorm is included in both the generator and the discriminator.

- Fully connected hidden layers areremoved for deeper architectures.

- ReLU activation is used in a generator for all layers except for the output, which uses Tanh.

- A new concept `LeakyReLU` activation in the discriminator for all layers.

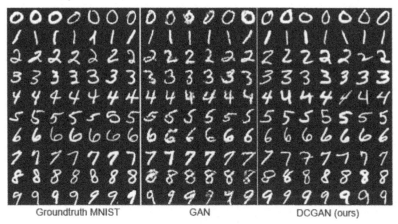

Groundtruth MNIST   GAN   DCGAN (ours)

Figure 4.9

The generator

In the generator, we use `tf.keras.layers.Conv2DTranspose` layers for upsampling to produce an image from noise called as **seed**. After that dense layer is used that takes seed as input, then upsample several times until you reach the desired image size of 28x28x1.We will use `tf.keras.layers.LeakyReLU` activation for each layer except the output layer where we will use tanh function.

```
1   def make_generator_model():
2       model = tf.keras.Sequential()
3       model.add(layers.Dense(7*7*256, use_bias=False, input_shape=(100,)))
4       model.add(layers.BatchNormalization())
5       model.add(layers.LeakyReLU())
6
7       model.add(layers.Reshape((7, 7, 256)))
8       assert model.output_shape == (None, 7, 7, 256) # Note: None is the batch size
9
10      model.add(layers.Conv2DTranspose(128, (5, 5), strides=(1, 1), padding='same', use_bias=False))
11      assert model.output_shape == (None, 7, 7, 128)
12      model.add(layers.BatchNormalization())
13      model.add(layers.LeakyReLU())
14
15      model.add(layers.Conv2DTranspose(64, (5, 5), strides=(2, 2), padding='same', use_bias=False))
16      assert model.output_shape == (None, 14, 14, 64)
17      model.add(layers.BatchNormalization())
18      model.add(layers.LeakyReLU())
19
20
21      model.add(layers.Conv2DTranspose(1, (5, 5), strides=(2, 2), padding='same', use_bias=False, activation='tanh'))
22      assert model.output_shape == (None, 28, 28, 1)
23
24      return model
```

Figure 4.10

The discriminator

A CNN -based image classifier which used to classify images as real or fake.For fake image, it produces output as negative values and for real images produces positive values.

```
1   def make_discriminator_model():
2       model = tf.keras.Sequential()
3       model.add(layers.Conv2D(64, (5, 5), strides=(2, 2), padding='same',
4                               input_shape=[28, 28, 1]))
5       model.add(layers.LeakyReLU())
6       model.add(layers.Dropout(0.3))
7
8       model.add(layers.Conv2D(128, (5, 5), strides=(2, 2), padding='same'))
9       model.add(layers.LeakyReLU())
10      model.add(layers.Dropout(0.3))
11
12      model.add(layers.Flatten())
13      model.add(layers.Dense(1))
14
15      return model
```

Figure 4.11

Applications

- The generation of animated characters
- Dataset augmentation

InfoGAN

Defining InfoGAN, it uses information theory concept to transform some of the noise terms into latent codes that have systematic, predictable effects on the outcome.

The traditional noise vector and a new latent code vector. The codes are then made meaningful by maximizing the Mutual Informationbetween the code and the generator output.

Info GAN is an Information theory combined with GAN and learns the representation of latent variables (variables that are not developed or concealed till now) even it can change handwriting fashions.It is unsupervised learning which extracts information from data which is not labelled. It uses GAN's by maximizing mutual information of datasets(many datasets found having mutual latent information as a variable).

GANobjective functionis min-max function, but it can't use mutual information from latent variables.

Like in MNIST dataset model can have a latent variable as that represents digit with encodes handwritten style. In InfoGAN, the generator provides latent variables and noise, the mutual information between latent code and generator distribution, and maximize it.Means if the latent variable is observed, reduce the uncertainty of real variable input needed to the generator.To extract mutual information between digitsis hard, but we can optimize the lower bound between the digits.This is called as **variational information maximization.**

Lemma is provided to extract lower bound between the latent variable and generator distribution.In Info GAN, we introduce negligible conditioning cost as compared to GAN. We have to maximize Mutual Information.In response, we have to maximize the lower bound.Without regularization, we can't maximize MI.

How to detangle (remove the knot from …) styles from digit: Capture variation of data while capturing a style of digit data.Latent variables will be digits or style or rotation,and so on.

Coding in InfoGAN

It is a approach in which we divide the generator input into two parts:

- Noise vector
- Latent code vector

After that code is made meaningful by maximizing mutual information between the code and generator output.

```
def generator(z, c):
    inputs = tf.concat(axis=1, values=[z, c])
    G_h1 = tf.nn.relu(tf.matmul(inputs, G_W1) + G_b1)
    G_log_prob = tf.matmul(G_h1, G_W2) + G_b2
    G_prob = tf.nn.sigmoid(G_log_prob)


return G_prob
```

Theory

This framework is implemented by merely adding a regularization term (red box) to theoriginal GAN's objective function.

$$\min_{G} \max_{D} V_I(D, G) = V(D, G) \boxed{- \lambda I(c; G(z, c))}$$

Figure 4.12

Lambda is the regularization constant and is typically just set to one. The $I(c; G(z,c))$ term is the mutual information between the latent code c and the generator output $G(z,c)$.

By using standard variational arguments, we calculate mutual information. This consists of introducing an auxiliary distribution $Q(c|x)$, which is modelled by a parameterized neural network and is meant to approximate the real $P(c|x)$. $P(c|x)$ represents the likelihood of code c given the generated input x. Then we use re-parameterization trick to make it such that user can use a sample from a user-specified prior (that is, uniform distribution) instead of the unknown posterior.

$$L_I(G,Q) = \boxed{E_{c\sim P(c)} \underbrace{x\sim G(z,c)}[\log Q(c|x)]} + \boxed{H(c)}$$
$$= E_{x\sim G(z,c)}[E_{c'\sim P(c|x)}[\log Q(c'|x)]] + H(c)$$
$$\leq I(c; G(z,c))$$

Prior = Easy!

Constant, not important

Posterior = Hard

Figure 4.13

$$L_I(G,Q) = E_{c\sim P(c), x\sim G(z,c)}[\log Q(c|x)] + H(c)$$

Figure 4.14

The regularizer term precedingtranslates to the following process: Sample value for the latent code c and noise z from a prior of your choice.

Generate $x = G(c,z)$; Calculate $Q(c \mid x = G(c,z))$.

The final objective function is then given by this lower-bound approximation to the mutual information:

$$\min_{G,Q} \max_{D} V_{\text{InfoGAN}}(D,G,Q) = V(D,G) - \lambda L_I(G,Q)$$

Figure 4.15

Architecture

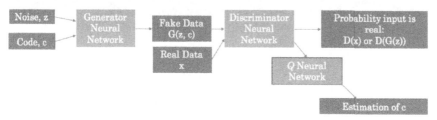

Figure 4.16

Now a second input to the generator - the latent code. The auxiliary distribution is modelled by another neural network, which is just a fully connected layer tacked onto the last representation layer of the discriminator. The Q network is essentially trying to predict what the code is. Q is used when feeding in fake input since that's the only time the code is known.

Table 1: The discriminator and generator CNNs used for MNIST dataset.

discriminator D / recognition network Q	generator G
Input 28 × 28 Gray image	Input $\in \mathbb{R}^{74}$
4 × 4 conv. 64 IRELU. stride 2	FC. 1024 RELU. batchnorm
4 × 4 conv. 128 IRELU. stride 2. batchnorm	FC. 7 × 7 × 128 RELU. batchnorm
FC. 1024 IRELU. batchnorm	4 × 4 upconv. 64 RELU. stride 2. batchnorm
FC. output layer for D, FC.128-batchnorm-IRELU-FC.output for Q	4 × 4 upconv. 1 channel

Figure 4.17

Results

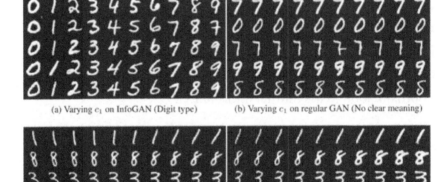

(a) Varying c_1 on InfoGAN (Digit type) (b) Varying c_1 on regular GAN (No clear meaning)

(c) Varying c_2 from −2 to 2 on InfoGAN (Rotation) (d) Varying c_3 from −2 to 2 on InfoGAN (Width)

Figure 4.18

Comparing InfoGAN to regular GAN when changing code values. From InfoGAN paper.

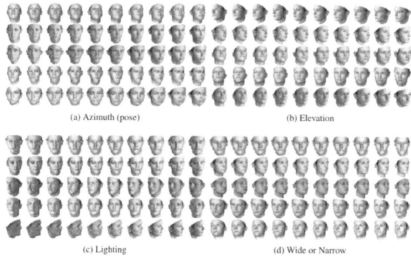

(a) Azimuth (pose)　　　　　　　　　(b) Elevation

(c) Lighting　　　　　　　　　(d) Wide or Narrow

Figure 4.19

Results on 3D face model dataset

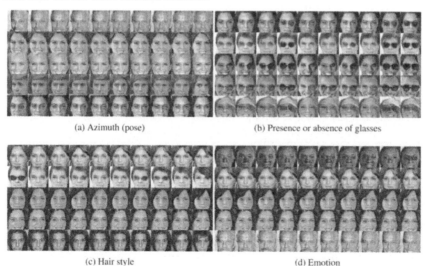

(a) Azimuth (pose)　　　　　　　　　(b) Presence or absence of glasses

(c) Hair style　　　　　　　　　(d) Emotion

Figure 4.20: Results on CelebA dataset

Pix2Pix

Pix2pix GAN in which it takes one pixel in the input image and converts it into output image pixel.

Components of Pix2Pix model

- Training data pair (*x* and *y*, where *x* is the input image and *y* is the output image):

```
x = tf.placeholder(tf.float32, shape=(None, img_size, img_size, channels))
y = tf.placeholder(tf.float32, shape=(None, img_size, img_size, channels))
```

Figure 4.21

- Pix2Pix model uses conditional GAN (cGAN) G: {x, z} → y. (z → noise vector, x → input image, y → output image)

- Generator network (encode-decode architecture) as an image is an input:

```
def generator(x, isTrain=True, reuse=False):

    with tf.variable_scope('generator', reuse=reuse):

        # encoder
        conv1 = lrelu(tf.layers.conv2d(x, 64, [4, 4], strides=(2, 2), padding='same', kernel_initializer=w_init,
        conv2 = lrelu(tf.layers.batch_normalization(tf.layers.conv2d(conv1, 128, [4, 4], strides=(2, 2), padding
        conv3 = lrelu(tf.layers.batch_normalization(tf.layers.conv2d(conv2, 256, [4, 4], strides=(2, 2), padding
        conv4 = lrelu(tf.layers.batch_normalization(tf.layers.conv2d(conv3, 512, [4, 4], strides=(2, 2), padding
        conv5 = lrelu(tf.layers.batch_normalization(tf.layers.conv2d(conv4, 512, [4, 4], strides=(2, 2), padding
        conv6 = lrelu(tf.layers.batch_normalization(tf.layers.conv2d(conv5, 512, [4, 4], strides=(2, 2), padding
        conv7 = lrelu(tf.layers.batch_normalization(tf.layers.conv2d(conv6, 512, [4, 4], strides=(2, 2), padding
        conv8 = tf.nn.relu(tf.layers.conv2d(conv7, 512, [4, 4], strides=(2, 2), padding='same', kernel_initializ

        # decoder and skip connections
        deconv1 = tf.nn.dropout(tf.layers.batch_normalization(tf.layers.conv2d_transpose(conv8, 512, [4, 4], str
        deconv1 = tf.nn.relu(tf.concat([deconv1, conv7], 3))

        deconv2 = tf.nn.dropout(tf.layers.batch_normalization(tf.layers.conv2d_transpose(deconv1, 512, [4, 4], s
        deconv2 = tf.nn.relu(tf.concat([deconv2, conv6], 3))

        deconv3 = tf.nn.dropout(tf.layers.batch_normalization(tf.layers.conv2d_transpose(deconv2, 512, [4, 4], s
        deconv3 = tf.nn.relu(tf.concat([deconv3, conv5], 3))

        deconv4 = tf.layers.batch_normalization(tf.layers.conv2d_transpose(deconv3, 512, [4, 4], strides=(2, 2),
        deconv4 = tf.nn.relu(tf.concat([deconv4, conv4], 3))

        deconv5 = tf.layers.batch_normalization(tf.layers.conv2d_transpose(deconv4, 256, [4, 4], strides=(2, 2),
        deconv5 = tf.nn.relu(tf.concat([deconv5, conv3], 3))

        deconv6 = tf.layers.batch_normalization(tf.layers.conv2d_transpose(deconv5, 128, [4, 4], strides=(2, 2),
        deconv6 = tf.nn.relu(tf.concat([deconv6, conv2], 3))

        deconv7 = tf.layers.batch_normalization(tf.layers.conv2d_transpose(deconv6, 64, [4, 4], strides=(2, 2),
        deconv7 = tf.nn.relu(tf.concat([deconv7, conv1], 3))

        deconv8 = tf.nn.tanh(tf.layers.conv2d_transpose(deconv7, 3, [4, 4], strides=(2, 2), padding='same', kerr

    return deconv8
```

Figure 4.22

- In the discriminator network, we will use patchGAN:

```
def discriminator(x, y, isTrain=True, reuse=False):

    with tf.variable_scope('discriminator', reuse=reuse):

        cat1 = tf.concat([x, y], 3)
        conv1 = lrelu(tf.layers.conv2d(cat1, 64, [4, 4], strides=(2, 2), padding='same', kernel_initializer=w_in
        conv2 = lrelu(tf.layers.batch_normalization(tf.layers.conv2d(conv1, 128, [4, 4], strides=(2, 2), padding

        conv3 = tf.layers.batch_normalization(tf.layers.conv2d(conv2, 256, [4, 4], strides=(2, 2), padding='same
        conv3 = lrelu(tf.pad(conv3, [[0, 0], [1, 1], [1, 1], [0, 0]], mode="CONSTANT"))

        conv4 = tf.layers.batch_normalization(tf.layers.conv2d(conv3, 512, [4, 4], strides=(1, 1), padding='vali
        conv4 = lrelu(tf.pad(conv4, [[0, 0], [1, 1], [1, 1], [0, 0]], mode="CONSTANT"))

        conv5 = tf.layers.conv2d(conv4, 1, [4, 4], strides=(1, 1), padding='valid', kernel_initializer=w_init, b

        out = tf.nn.sigmoid(conv5) #gives 30*30 patchGAN

        return out, conv5
```

Figure 4.23

- CGAN loss function (L1 or L2 distance):

$$\mathcal{L}_{cGAN}(G, D) = \mathbb{E}_{x,y}[\log D(x, y)] + \mathbb{E}_{x,z}[\log(1 - D(x, G(x, z)))],$$

$$\mathcal{L}_{L1}(G) = \mathbb{E}_{x,y,z}[\|y - G(x, z)\|_1]. \qquad \mathcal{L}_{L2}(G) = \mathbb{E}_{x,y,z}(y - G(x, z))^2$$

Figure 4.24

```
G_x = generator(x)
D_real_outputs, D_real_logits = discriminator(x, y)
D_fake_outputs, D_fake_logits = discriminator(x, G_x, reuse=True)

D_loss_real = tf.reduce_mean(tf.nn.sigmoid_cross_entropy_with_logits(logits=D_real_logits,
                                          labels=tf.ones_like(D_real_logits)))
D_loss_fake = tf.reduce_mean(tf.nn.sigmoid_cross_entropy_with_logits(logits=D_fake_logits,
                                          labels=tf.zeros_like(D_fake_logits)))
D_loss = (D_loss_real + D_loss_fake)

G_loss_gan = tf.reduce_mean(tf.nn.sigmoid_cross_entropy_with_logits(logits=D_fake_logits,
                                          labels=tf.ones_like(D_fake_logits)))
G_l1_loss = tf.reduce_mean(tf.reduce_sum(tf.abs(G_x - y), 3))

G_loss = G_loss_gan + G_l1_loss * l1_weight
```

Figure 4.25

- Generator G tries to output an image from input noise and input image close to real image so that discriminator cannot distinguish it.

- Discriminator D tries to classify between real and fake image.

- Generator G not only trying to reduce loss from discriminator but also create a fake image so real that discriminator cannot discriminate.

- The loss function of the generator layer is:

$$G^* = \arg \min_G \max_D \mathcal{L}_{cGAN}(G, D) + \lambda \mathcal{L}_{L1}(G).$$

Figure 4.26

- Training duration:

```
for it in range(200):
    epoch_start_time = time.time()
    for iter in range(train.shape[0] // batch_size):
        train_data = train.next_batch()
        train_x = norm(train_data[:, :, img_size:, :])
        train_y = norm(train_data[:, :, 0:img_size, :])
        _, D_loss_curr = sess.run([D_solver, D_loss], feed_dict={x: train_x, y: train_y})
        _, G_loss_curr = sess.run([G_solver, G_loss], feed_dict={x: train_x, y: train_y})
```

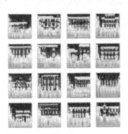

Epoch 1

```
Iter: 0
D loss: 0.3862
G loss: 114.4

The total time for epoch0 is49.39186334609985
```

Figure 4.27

Architecture

Generator

The U-Net structure is used as an encoder-decoder in generator block.

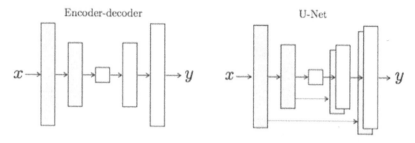

Figure 4.28

Discriminator

Discriminator takes two jobs on an input image and an unknown image and also decide if another image is produced by generator or not. Discriminator uses PatchGAN (N*N model) works pixel-wise instead of saying the whole image is fake it process every pixel and tell if real or fake.

Results

Figure 4.29: Cityscapes labels->photo, compared to ground truth

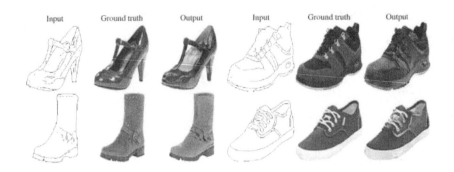

Figure 4.30: *Automatically detected edges -> shoes, compared to ground truth*

pix2pix application

pix2pix can be used for the image to image translation such as

- Image to segmented images or vice versa
- Aerial photo to map or vice versa
- Grayscale image to color photos.
- Edges to photo.
- Sketch to photo

PAN

In April 2019, **perceptual adversarial networks (PAN)** were introduced: It is also aimed at the image to image translation. PAN combines the generative adversarial loss(the generative adversarial loss acts as a statistical measurement to penalize the discrepancy between the distributions of transformed images and the ground-truth images) and the proposed perceptual adversarial loss(perceptual adversarial loss directly measures and minimizes differences between generated images and ground-truth images from different perspectives) as a novel training loss function.

PAN consists of an image transformation network T, and a discriminative network D. The image transformation network T is trained to synthesize the transformed images given the input images. It is composed of a stack of **Convolution-BatchNorm-LeakyReLU** encoding layers and **deconvolution-BatchNorm-ReLU** decoding layers, and the skip-connections are used between mirrored layers. The discriminative network D is also a CNN that consists of

Convolution-BatchNorm-LeakyReLU layers. Hidden layers of the network D are utilized to evaluate the perceptual adversarial loss, and the output of the network D is used to distinguish transformed images from real-world images.

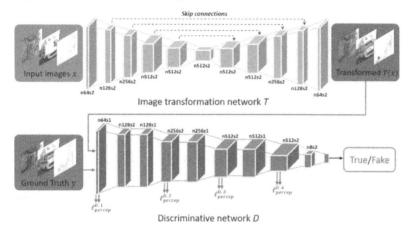

Figure 4.31

ID-CGAN

Image De-raining Conditional Generative Adversarial Network (ID-CGAN) was introduced in June 2019. It is used for the image to image translation.

Stack GAN

Conditioning augmentation

First test description t is encoded by encoder yielding a text embedding φ_t.Conditioning augmentation is used to produce additional conditioning variables ^c.After φ_t we will pass it to Gaussian distribution wherethe mean and diagonal covariance matrix is the function of φ_t to capture the meaning of φ_t with variations.The conditioning augmentation will yield number of training pairs given a small number of image-text pairs. The randomness introduced in the conditioning augmentation is beneficial for modelling text to image translation as the same sentence usually corresponds to objects with various poses and appearances.To avoid overfitting condition, we use **Kullback-Leibler divergence (KL divergence)** to the objective of the generator during the training.

Stage I

This stage focuses on extracting drawing the only rough shape and correct colors for the object.

For generator G_0 if we have a text we will convert it into text embedding vector then pass it to fully connected layer to generate the mean and the standard deviation for Gaussian distribution. $^\wedge c_0$ are then sampled from Gaussian distribution which is of N_g dimensional vector after that it is concatenated with N_z dimensional noise vector to generate $W_0 \times H_0$ image by series of upsampling blocks.

For the discriminator D_0, the text embedding φ_t is first compressed to N_d dimensions using a fully-connected layer and then spatially replicated to form a $M_d \times M_d \times N_d$ tensor. Then it goes througha series of down-sampling blocks until it has $M_d \times M_d$ spatial dimension. Having gone through other transformation,a fully connected layer with one node is used to produce the decision score.

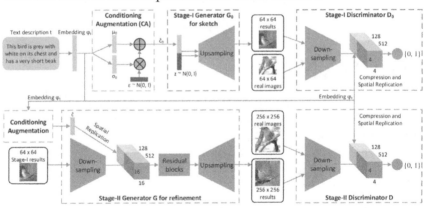

Figure 4.32

Stage II

The Stage-II GAN uses earlier missed info to generate more photo-realistic details. Gaussian conditioning variable in *Stage-I* and *Stage-II* both share same pre-trained text encoder, generating the same text embedding φ_t.

Cycle GAN

To resolve the problem of image-to-image translation in case where you don't have paired training samples. Our model contains two mapping functions $G : X \rightarrow Y$ and $F : Y \rightarrow X$, and associated adversarial discriminators D_x and D_y. D_y encourages G to translate X into outputs indistinguishable from domain Y, and vice versa for D_x and F. To further regularize the mappings, we introduce two-cycle consistency losses that capture the intuition that if we translate from one domain to the other, and back again we should arrive at where we started: (b) forward cycle-consistency loss: $x \rightarrow G(x) \rightarrow F(G(x)) \approx x$, and *(c)* backward cycle-consistency loss: $y \rightarrow F(y) \rightarrow G(F(y)) \approx y$.

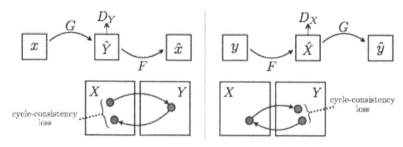

Figure 4.33

CycleGAN transfers styles to images

For example, we start with collecting three sets of pictures: one for real scenery, one for Monet paintings and the last one for Van Gogh. Can we take a real picture and transfer the style of Monet or Van Gogh onto it? On the other hand, can we make a Monet picture looks real?

It transforms the picture from one domain to another domain. To transform pictures between real images and Van Gogh paintings. We build three networks.

- A generator G to convert an image from real to Von Gogh paintings
- A generator F to convert an image from Von Gogh painting to real
- A discriminator D to identify real or Von Gogh painting

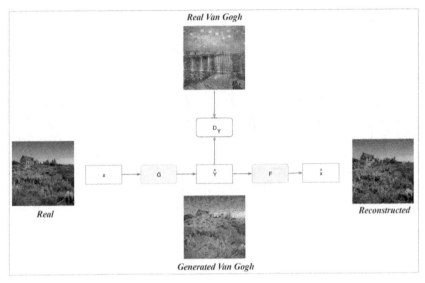

Figure 4.34

For the reverse direction, we just reverse the data flow and build an additional discriminator D_X to identify real images.

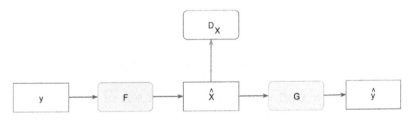

Figure 4.35

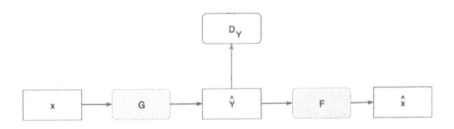

Figure 4.36

Coding implementation:

```
y_fake = generator(x,scope='G_x2y') # x --> G(x) --> y'
x_fake = generator(y, scope='G_y2x') # y --> F(y) --> x'

#should be getting same as x and y
x_cycle = generator(y_fake,reuse=True,scope='G_y2x') # x --> G(x) --> y' --> F(y') = x
y_cycle = generator(x_fake,reuse=True,scope='G_x2y') # y --> F(y) --> x' --> G(x') = y

DX_real = discriminator(x,scope='DX')
DY_real = discriminator(y,scope='DY')
DX_fake = discriminator(x_fake, reuse=True,scope='DX')
DY_fake = discriminator(y_fake, reuse=True,scope='DY')

# Discriminator Loss (we use LSGAN loss)
Gan_loss_DX = (tf.reduce_mean(tf.square(DX_real - tf.ones_like(DX_real))) +
               tf.reduce_mean(tf.square(DX_fake)))/ 2.0
Gan_loss_DY = (tf.reduce_mean(tf.square(DY_real - tf.ones_like(DY_real))) +
               tf.reduce_mean(tf.square(DY_fake))) / 2.0

# Cycle consistent Loss
l1 = 10
cycle_loss = tf.reduce_mean(l1 * tf.abs(x - x_cycle)) + tf.reduce_mean(l1 * tf.abs(y - y_cycle))

# Generator Loss
Gan_loss_GX = tf.reduce_mean(tf.square(DY_fake - tf.ones_like(DY_fake))) + cycle_loss
Gan_loss_FY = tf.reduce_mean(tf.square(DX_fake - tf.ones_like(DX_fake))) + cycle_loss
```

· tf.trainable_variables() D_X_vars = [v for v in training_vars if v.name.startswith('D_X')] D_Y_vars = [v for v in training_vars if with('D_Y')] G_xy_vars = [v for v in training_vars if v.name.startswith('G_x2y')] G_yx_vars = [v for v in training_vars if with('G_y2x')]

```
DX_vars = tf.get_collection(tf.GraphKeys.TRAINABLE_VARIABLES, 'DX')
DY_vars = tf.get_collection(tf.GraphKeys.TRAINABLE_VARIABLES, 'DY')
G_x2y_vars = tf.get_collection(tf.GraphKeys.TRAINABLE_VARIABLES, 'G_x2y')
G_y2x_vars = tf.get_collection(tf.GraphKeys.TRAINABLE_VARIABLES, 'G_y2x')

DX_solver = tf.train.AdamOptimizer(learning_rate=learning_rate).minimize(Gan_loss_DX, var_list=DX_vars)
DY_solver = tf.train.AdamOptimizer(learning_rate=learning_rate).minimize(Gan_loss_DY, var_list=DY_vars)
G_x2y_solver = tf.train.AdamOptimizer(learning_rate=learning_rate).minimize(Gan_loss_GX, var_list=G_x2y_va
rs)
G_y2x_solver = tf.train.AdamOptimizer(learning_rate=learning_rate).minimize(Gan_loss_FY, var_list=G_y2x_va
rs)

sess = tf.InteractiveSession()
tf.global_variables_initializer().run()
```

Figure 4.37

Style GAN

GAN is having so many challenges in output from random noise input such as changing specific features such as pose, face shape and hairstyle in an image of a face.Style GAN generates artificial images from low resolution continuing to high resolution (1024x1024). It is achieved by modifying input of each level, and it controls visual features that are expressed in that level, such as (pose,facial expression) continuing to (hair color) without affecting other levels. It generates more authenticated images as compared to previous GAN output.

The basic component of every GAN is a generator and discriminatory, andthe generator generates images from scratch and discriminator discriminate between fake and real having input generated images and training data. Overtime generator receives its input as feedback from the discriminatory.

Style GAN uses the concept of ProGAN with a focus on the generator network.Style GAN divides the feature for three types:

- **Coarse:** Resolution of up to 82 - effects pose, general hairstyle, face shape, and so on.

- **Middle:** Resolution of 162 to 322 - affects finer facial features, hairstyle, eyes open/closed, and so on.

- **Fine:** Resolution of 642 to 10242 - affects color scheme (eye, hair and skin) and micro features.

Mapping network

When we are passing input training data into the generator, it has to follow the probability density of training data, so thedegree of freedom is less to consider other visual features to produce a fine image.This limitation is called as **feature entanglement**.To deal with this difficulty, we are introducing a mapping network to encode input vector to an intermediate vector to consider other visual feature.For that, we are using 8 fully connected layer network.By using another neural network,we are not limited tothe distribution of training data.

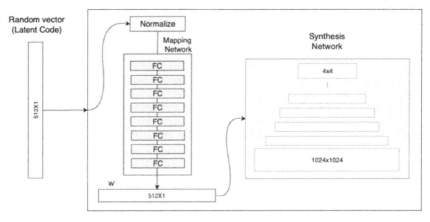

Figure 4.38

Style modules (AdaIN)

AdaIN translates encoded w information created by mapping network into the generated images. The module is added to each resolution level of the synthesis network and defines the visual expression of the features in that level:

1. Each channel of the convolution layer output is first normalized to make sure the scaling and shifting of *step 3* have the expected effect.

2. The intermediate vector w is transformed using another fully-connected layer (marked as A) into a scale and bias for each channel.

3. The scale and bias vectors shift each channel of the convolution output, thereby defining the importance of each filter in the convolution. This tuning translates the information from w to a visual representation.

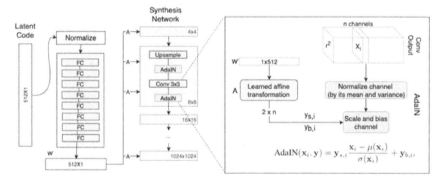

Figure 4.39

Removing initial input

The StyleGAN team found that the image features are controlled by w and the AdaIN, and therefore the initial input can be omitted and replaced by constant values.

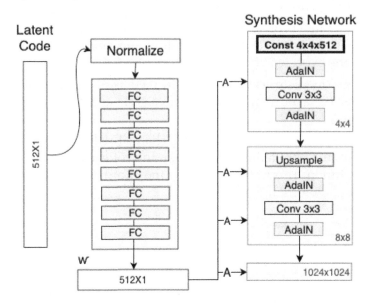

Figure 4.40

Stochastic variation

There are many aspects in people's faces that are small and can be seen as stochastic, such as freckles, the exact placement of hairs, wrinkles, features which make the image more realistic and increase the variety of outputs. The common method to insert these small features into GAN images is adding random noise to the input vector.

The noise in StyleGAN is added in a similar way to the AdaIN mechanism—a scaled noise is added to each channel before the

AdaIN module and changes a bit the visual expression of the features of the resolution level it operates on.

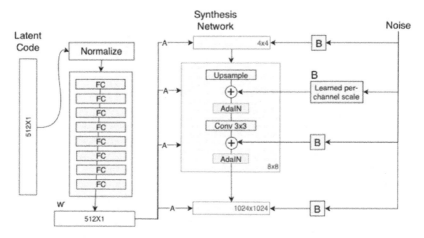

Figure 4.41

Style mixing

The model generates two images *A* and *B* and then combines them by taking low-level features from *A* and the rest of the features from *B*.

Truncation trick in W

The major challenge in the generator is it generates bad looking images.To avoid generating poor images, StyleGAN truncates the intermediate vector *w*, forcing it to stay close to the average intermediate vector.

When generating new images, instead of using mapping network output directly, *w* is transformed into *w*_new=*w*_avg+ψ(*w* -*w*_avg), where the value of ψ defines how far the image can be from the average image (and how diverse the output can be). Interestingly, by using a different ψ for each level, before the affine transformation block, the model can control how far from average each set of features is:

- **Fine-tuning:** Additional improvement of StyleGAN upon ProGAN was updating several network hyperparameters, such as training duration and loss function, and replacing the up/downscaling from nearest neighbours to bilinear sampling. Though this step is significant for the model performance, it's less innovative and therefore won't be described here in detail:

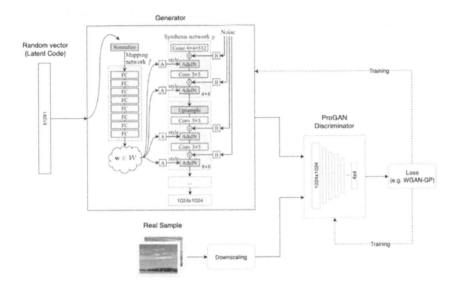

Figure 4.42

Radial GAN

Radial GAN is used for numerical analysis. If we are considering an object and collecting numerical data from various sources.They estimate in a different environment and different aspects.Radial GAN transforms each sources data in latent space to convert it in a uniform format.Then we convert latent space data into feature space data of each unique dataset.

Each dataset in the Radial GAN converted latent dataset to features dataset.Each Radial GAN has encoder which converts the dataset as latent space dataset.Each dataset has decoder also which discriminate whether the latent dataset information is aligned with target dataset.

The same process is used for all the sources dataset.Inthe end, we append all the information to target dataset information.In each dataset, we are passing information through the encoder to latent space which passes it to the decoder.

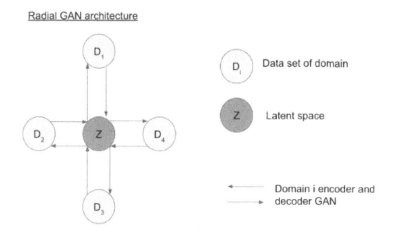

Figure 4.43

Conclusion

The present chapter includes machine learning technique GAN, its architectural concept.

It gives the reader a clear picture of various types of GAN model introduced for solving various problems of our day to day life like image to image generator, image to text generator,and so on.

The reader can get in-depth knowledge of techniques by their architectural design, creating model, training, and final step through results.

The end of the chapter will provide readers with information about pix2pix technique deeply as it is an important Part of GAN.

A hoping reader can satisfy their hunger of knowledge about GAN through this chapter workflow.

Exercise

1. What are the interesting factors behind creating GAN?

2. List various types of GAN techniques

3. Why is pix2pix preferred other than techniques in GAN?

4. If you have a flower image, how will you convert it into text information?

5. In DCGAN output layer used different activation function, which functions are used throughout and at the output layer?

6. List all applications of cGAN

Made in the USA
Coppell, TX
18 August 2021

60700483R00075